Praise for *In*

C000147730

'It's like sitting down and getting advice from a clear thinking friend who steers me towards focusing on the results I want. I am recommending this book to…valued business professionals I know who will definately benefit from reading it.'

Hilary Dustan, Learning and Development Director, Black & Decker

'The skills in this book are basic, but potent. I am heartened to see the mechanics of impactful communication laid out in a way that can be easily utilised in all areas of your life. When you use the skills taught in the pages of this book … the world will open up to you.'

Peta Haskell, Relationship Guide, Author of Flirt Coach

'Personal impact can be learnt and this book teaches you how to get it. Full of useful exercises and practical tips it will help you achieve success in both your career and personal life.'

Robbie Steinhouse, Entrepreneur and Author of Think Like an Entrepreneur

'In an age where success depends more on persuasion and influence than knowledge, this book is a welcome companion. The easy to follow structure takes you through the stages of inner confidence and self-belief, giving you ideas and tools to develop positive personal impact. Buy this book, do the exercises, and you will definitely feel the change.'

David Molden, NLP Trainer, Coach, Author of Managing with the Power of NLP

'This book is the A to Z for being memorable and attractive, from creating your first impressions to building lasting relationships. *Impact* contains an incredible number of ideas for how to increase your impact with individuals and whole groups of people.'

Shelle Rose Charvet, Facilitator and Author of **Words That Change Minds**

'This book skilfully blends simplicity and intelligence. The thoughts are clearly expressed, but the wisdom is palpably distilled from thousands of encounters, formal and informal, and from the ability to weave together something as learned as Carl Jung's teachings with something as simple as telling you to smile more – and watch the response!'

Alison Smale, Managing Editor, **International Herald Tribune**

'An essential guide to the art and science of impression management.'

Dr Peter Collett, Author of **Book of Tells**

'Packed with useful tools and ideas – a personal impact book with real impact.'

Wayne Mullen, Head of Learning and Development, Standard Bank

'This book can make a huge difference in your life – minimum intervention for maximum result.'

Sue Knight, Author of **NLP at Work**

Impact

Prentice Hall LIFE

If life is what you make it, then making it better starts here.

What we learn today can change our lives tomorrow. It can change our goals or change our minds; open up new opportunities or simply inspire us to make a difference. That's why we have created a new breed of books that do more to help you make more of *your* life.

Whether you want more confidence or less stress, a new skill or a different perspective, we've designed *Prentice Hall Life* books to help you to make a change for the better. Together with our authors we share a commitment to bring you the brightest ideas and best ways to manage your life, work and wealth.

In these pages we hope you'll find the ideas you need for the life *you* want. Go on, help yourself.

It's what you make it

* * *

Impact

Impress your way to success

Amanda Vickers, Steve Bavister and Jackie Smith

Prentice Hall Life
is an imprint of

Harlow, England • London • New York • Boston • San Francisco • Toronto
Sydney • Tokyo • Singapore • Hong Kong • Seoul • Taipei • New Delhi
Cape Town • Madrid • Mexico City • Amsterdam • Munich • Paris • Milan

PEARSON EDUCATION LIMITED

Edinburgh Gate
Harlow CM20 2JE
Tel: +44 (0)1279 623623
Fax: +44 (0)1279 431059
Website: www.pearson.com/uk

First published in Great Britain in 2009 as *Personal Impact*
Second edition published as *Impact* in 2012

ISBN: 978-0-273-76161-7

British Library Cataloguing-in-Publication Data
A catalogue record for this book is available from the British Library

Library of Congress Cataloging-in-Publication Data
Vickers, Amanda.
 Impact : impress your way to success : discover and clarify your purpose / Amanda
Vickers, Steve Bavister, and Jackie Smith. -- 2nd ed.
  p. cm.
 Rev. ed. of: Personal impact. c2009.
 ISBN 978-0-273-76161-7 (pbk.)
 1. Success in business. 2. Self-perception. 3. Interpersonal relations. I. Bavister, Steve.
II. Smith, Jackie. III. Vickers, Amanda. Personal impact. IV. Title.
 HF5386.V53 2012
 650.1--dc23
                                2011036364

10 9 8 7 6 5 4 3 2 1
15 14 13 12 11

Cartoons by Viv Mullett
Typeset in 10/14 Plantin by 30
Printed in Great Britain by Henry Ling Ltd., at the Dorset Press, Dorchester, Dorset

Contents

Acknowledgements

We want to start by saying 'thank you' to all those who have attended a Speak First course over the years. You made this book possible. We learnt so much from you that we were inspired to share our insights with a wider audience. In the beginning we thought we were teaching you, but actually it was the other way round. You are the real authors of *Impact*. Every workshop we've run has given us a deeper, richer understanding of the subject. It has been a privilege and a pleasure to work with each and every one of you. Thank you.

Our special thanks go to the publishing team at Pearson who nurtured this book from concept to completion. In particular we'd like to acknowledge the contribution of Sam Jackson, whose advice, insight and feedback have proved invaluable, and of Caroline Jordan and Laura Blake whose professionalism and patience have been central to making this book a success.

Without the dedication of the staff at Speak First this book would never have seen the light of day. Thanks for doing such a fantastic job of holding the fort while we were busy writing. You're all great examples of people who make an impact every single day.

To our families, who have barely seen us during the months it took to complete the manuscript, we appreciate your continued support and understanding. Special thanks go to Amanda's mum, Joyce Vickers, who provided her with a 'bolt-hole' of peace and tranquility to get on with the book. 'I've learnt a lot about building great relationships with people from my mum over the years,' says Amanda, 'and I owe her a huge debt of thanks.' Thanks also to Caitlyn Gray, Amanda's niece, who is a shining light in her life. Jackie would like to thank her parents, Meg and Hugo Pigou – 'Your unwavering support and positive outlook made a huge difference in keeping me on track. You are excellent role models and have also helped me find my voice.' That just leaves Helen and Jack Bavister who continue to be an inspiration to their dear old dad in everything they do: 'You taught me so much.'

Impact is at the heart of the courses we run at Speak First – courses that include presenting, meeting the media, influencing, networking, business writing and, of course, personal impact itself. We would like to acknowledge the tremendous contribution of our consultants, current and past, who do a great job every day in delivering first-class training for our clients.

Thanks are also owed to our clients – too many to mention here – who recognise the importance of personal impact and place their trust in Speak First to help their people achieve success in every area of their working lives.

Finally, thanks are due to the many individuals who have inspired us and helped to shape our thinking, both in person and through books and audio/video recordings. These include: Tim Gallwey, Robert Dilts, Wayne Dyer, Eric Berne, Susi Strang, Tom Peters, Charles Faulkner, Fritz Perls, Jean Baer, Nathaniel Branden, Faye Brauer, Steve de Shazer, Stephanie Burns, John Gray, Helena Cornelius, Stephen Covey, Chris Duffy, Steve Jobs, Tad James, Susan Jeffers, Carl Jung, Wendy Matthews, Kaye Remington, Gail Sheehy, Anthony Robbins, Manuel J Smith, Ian McDermott, Andy Thorburn, Kerrie Walshaw, Shelle Rose Charvet, Shakti Gawain, Richard Bandler and John Grinder, Carlos Castaneda, Milton Erickson, Derren Brown, Robert Cialdini, Albert Ellis and Jane Northam.

Introduction – the power of personal impact

You are always making an impact. Whatever you do, wherever you are. Even if you just sit in the corner and say nothing, you're making an impact. But is it the right impact?

Have you ever missed out on a job or promotion because you didn't make a positive impression? Would you like to be able to influence people better? Do you sometimes struggle to get your point across in meetings and one-to-ones? Would you like to be able to assert yourself more confidently? Do people remember your colleagues but forget you?

If you answered 'yes' to even one of those questions, you need to increase your personal impact.

Why you need it

We live in an age where you need to have impact to be successful. It is the 'difference that makes the difference' when it comes to achieving what you want in life. No man, or woman, is an island. You need other people, and impact is interpersonal. It is something you have – something you do – in relation to others. You cannot have impact when you are on your own. When you are able to connect with people quickly and easily, win their trust and make a great impression on them, you are more likely to get what you want from the relationship.

The specific benefits of having personal impact are diverse and many, including:

- getting the job of your dreams

- earning more money

- influencing and persuading others

- meeting your soul mate

- impressing your boss

- having a fantastic network

- achieving your goals.

Your ability to achieve what you want in life depends to a large degree on the impact you have on others. Whether you like it or not, people size you up within seconds of meeting you; if you don't make a positive first impression you may not get another chance. These days people are so busy, so distracted – always multi-tasking, always thinking about emails – that it is harder than ever to make the right impact. Ultimately, having greater personal impact will mean you are taking charge of your life and will have more control over your own destiny.

When you need it

When do you need personal impact? *When do you not need it?* You need it all the time. Everywhere: at work and at play; in the office, factory, on location, or in the home. You need it to pass an interview, get your point across at meetings or to give an effective presentation. You may have a role in which you need to influence and persuade others – such as sales, negotiation and customer service – where making the right impact is vital for success.

People in all professions are becoming ever more aware that personal impact is a way of gaining a competitive edge over their rivals – and that without it they risk missing out on opportunities.

You will already have impact in some areas, and might want to enhance it, but you may have confidence or assertiveness issues in others which you would like to overcome. Perhaps this is because you have received feedback at work that suggests you need to develop your interpersonal skills to be able to move to the next level.

What is personal impact?

Personal impact is not easy to define, but we all know it when we see it. We meet someone and pretty soon we recognise they have a special quality. Call it magnetism, call it presence, call it charisma – call it what you like – but they stand out from the crowd.

Dictionary definitions of impact include:

- The force of impression of one thing on another.
- An effect or change caused by some factor.

That is what individuals with personal impact do: they make an impression on others, and through that they bring about some kind of change.

It is not about 'personality'

Some people think personal impact is all about having bags of 'personality'; of being the life and soul of the party, flamboyant and extrovert. But in the same way that a whisper can sometimes be louder than a shout, quiet introverted people – and even those who consider themselves 'shy' – can have personal impact that is every bit as powerful as those who are more 'out there'. It is not how you are, it is *who* you are. Ordinary people can make an extraordinary impact.

The optimum zone model

You can have too much of a good thing – and too little. There is an optimum range in which you will maximise your personal impact. Go outside that range and you reduce your impact. Lack of assertiveness almost always leads to negative impact – but so does too much, when it becomes aggression. The secret to success is getting it just right.

Too little	Optimum zone	Too much
1 2	3 4 5 6 7 8	9 10
Too quiet	Voice at just the right volume	Too loud
Static	Moves purposefully, deliberately	Restless movement
No gestures	Appropriate, relevant gestures	Frantic, random gestures
Too slow	Speed of delivery ideal	Pace too fast
Full of facts	Facts brought to life with examples	Just stories, no facts
Passive	Assertive	Aggressive
Charmless	Charming, persuasive	Cheesy, ingratiating

There is an optimum zone for many characteristics and behaviours in which personal impact is positive. Outside that zone – when there is too little or too much – impact is first reduced and ultimately turns negative.

Is it really possible to change the impact you make?

Absolutely. Many have done it, and you can do it. We are not talking about a complete makeover – the self-help equivalent of radical cosmetic surgery. Then it wouldn't be you.

Small changes, though, can lead to big results. Just softening your tone of voice or making it firmer, or increasing or reducing your eye contact can make a profound difference to the impact you have.

Impact is everything

Impact is *everything*. To be successful in life you need to be able to make an instant positive impression on others (even when they are busy or distracted), communicate powerfully with them, and to be persuasive and memorable.

Everyone can have impact if they want it – and know how to get it. That is what *Impact* will provide: techniques and strategies to take you from where you are to where you want to be. This book will change your life.

Chapter 1

Believe in yourself and boost your personal impact

'There's nothing on earth you cannot have – once you have mentally accepted the fact that you can have it.'

Robert Collier, bestselling self-help author

*P*icture the scene. At the tender age of nine, Lewis Hamilton walks up to Ron Dennis, the boss of McLaren, and tells him that one day he will drive for the team. How about that for self-belief? How about that for confidence? How about that for personal impact?

Lewis Hamilton clearly has the talent and determination to be a world-class Formula One driver, but it was his attitude that took him there. When you believe in yourself and set your sights on something, you are almost certain to make an impact.

The inner you creates the outer you

How you feel on the inside makes a huge difference to how you come across to others on the outside. That feeling shines through to the surface. You feel, look and sound confident and self-assured. You assertively ask for what you want, while respecting the needs and wants of other people. When you believe in yourself and think things are possible, they start to turn into reality. So much of your success is down to your attitude: it oils the wheels and makes it easy to achieve what you want, influence others and create an impact.

Many people who are sure of themselves tend to move and speak in a relaxed, unhurried fashion. While measured and composed most of the time, they are able to express their views with conviction and passion when they have an important point to make. Their outer behaviour is driven by inner factors such as self-belief, confidence, purpose and determination to succeed.

Believing in yourself creates personal impact

the more you can build your self-confidence and self-belief, the more successful you will be

While all of us have moments of insecurity, the more you can build your self-confidence and self-belief, the more successful you will be. Your thoughts and beliefs can be positive driving forces in your life. You remember a time when you convinced a colleague to implement an idea; this spurred you on to achieve your next goal. However, they can also act like brakes if you let them: you apply for a promotion, worry about blowing your own trumpet too much and end up underselling yourself. Once you recognise how to harness the power of your beliefs, there is no limit to the impact you can make.

Why is confidence important?

When you are confident everything feels easy and effortless. This is because you trust yourself to make an impact, so you appear natural to others; they feel safe in your hands, and they believe in what you say more readily. Because you are more assertive this means they are more likely to buy your ideas or products and implement your plans. People associate confidence with success. They gravitate in your direction, hoping some of it will rub off on them.

It feels good to you, too. The more confidence you have in different contexts, the more willing you are to take risks. You take on things you would otherwise not have dreamt possible.

What stops you being confident?

Lack of confidence comes down to one word: fear. Some people fear making a mistake, failing, or getting something wrong. Others are concerned about being rejected because they think they may come across as stupid or incompetent.

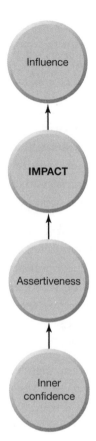

Confidence is central to impact

Feel the fear – but don't let it hold you back

When you lack confidence it stops you from trying to do things. But what would you try to do if you were a) not afraid of failing, and b) not worried about what others might think?

You would be willing to give it a go. Nothing bad could happen to you.

Imagine being free from doubt – totally believing in yourself and your abilities, without bragging or boasting. That is what it means to be confident. It is about self-belief and having faith in yourself.

It is also an emotional state. The word 'confidence' comes from the Latin *confidere* which means with (*con*) trust (*fidere*). The first step in projecting confidence is to trust yourself; if you don't, why should anyone else? Making an impact depends on it.

It sounds easy and – because of the way our brains work – it can be hard to pull off at times. As Geoff Thompson puts it in his book *Fear*, 'Working one's way through a life that is fraught with intangible confrontation, in an adrenal-loaded body that was designed for conflicts of a physical nature, it is small wonder that most people go to their graves with their best songs still in them.'

When we come across something that seems threatening – public speaking, walking into a room full of strangers, or something new we have not tried before – the 'reptilian' part of our brain prepares our body for 'fight', 'flight' or 'freezing stock still'. The hormones adrenaline and cortisol surge into the bloodstream and our heart rate increases. That same energy boost can spur us on to do a great job, run a marathon or deliver a fantastic speech.

Some people learn to hide fear well, like a swan sailing up a river with its little webbed feet working like crazy under the surface, or they simply do not think of it as being a threat. How you think about things you fear is the real key to overcoming anxiety. Those who are fearful have usually learnt to behave that way – perhaps they were asked to read something aloud at school and felt exposed.

 Exercise

On a scale of 1–10, where 1 is no confidence and 10 is extremely confident, where are you right now in relation to making an impact? What would it take to move you one or two places higher up the scale?

Monitor your response to this question over the coming weeks. Each time, become more aware of what increases your confidence level and what reduces it.

Case study: Richard Branson

Who do many budding entrepreneurs look to when formulating their plans for world domination? Richard Branson. He is the ultimate role model for thousands of aspiring business leaders: they want to *be* him. There is no denying the impact he has made, personally and professionally. He has started over 360 successful Virgin-branded companies, and at the last count he was the 263rd richest man on the planet. What excites people most about Richard Branson, though, is that he has done it his way. He has never been a 'suit', preferring to wear a jumper. His business and personal philosophy is arguably best summed up by the title of one his books: *Screw It, Let's Do It!*

How can you be more confident?

Here are some tried-and-tested ways of being more comfortable and confident.

- **Do it anyway – despite the fear**: Many of the confident people we come across in the world feel fearful when they do things for the first time. The best way to overcome your fears is through experience. The more networking events you go to, the easier it becomes. When you have attended a few large, high-profile meetings you start to know the ropes and feel increasingly at ease contributing.

  As Susan Jeffers says in her bestselling book *Feel the Fear and Do It Anyway*, 'Pushing through fear is less frightening than living with the underlying fear that comes with helplessness.' This statement may sound odd, but if you think about it, it is true.

  We protect ourselves from harm by not participating in something we are afraid of, and deep down know that, at some stage, we will have to face it. We can choose to stay paralysed or choose to break free. This is all about stretching your comfort zone. Once we develop our capability to do something our confidence grows.

- **Don't feel you have to do it or say it perfectly**: Do not expect to say things clearly every time. What you have to say may come out a bit muddled sometimes, and that is true for everyone. If you miss something out, you can always add it in later. If you get it slightly wrong, you can always clarify your point.

- **Learn to love the limelight or at least be able to tolerate it**: Many of us fantasise about what people will think of us and come to negative conclusions which fuel our anxieties. This is especially the case when we feel exposed or are put on the spot. You are asked to be available to answer questions on a plan you have proposed. You are afraid the committee will challenge you with all kinds of awkward questions and you will end up looking foolish if you don't know the answers. Realise that people are on your side and they have their own insecurities; they are all worrying about what other people are thinking about them too.

- **Be comfortable with conflict**: Although there is sometimes disagreement, and even conflict, this is rarely personal. Rather it is people arguing or fighting for causes they feel strongly about. Once you appreciate they are not 'having a go' at you, only challenging what you are saying, you can more confidently make suggestions and express opinions.

- **Focus on your strengths**: We tend to worry about our weaknesses. Often we're our own worst critic, minimising our successes and maximising our failures. When you run negative movies in your mind of how difficult things are and how inadequate you are to deal with them, it's small wonder you lose faith in your ability to conquer what has become Mount Everest. Instead, focus on your strengths and the times when you handled challenging situations well. Draw on the qualities you have already to succeed and make an impact.

● **Act as if you are already confident**: Acting as if you are already doing something you want to do can have a really powerful and positive effect. It acts like an accelerator that takes you down a fast track to where you want to be. When you 'act as if', you take on the mindset of what you want to become. If you practise long enough, your acting 'as if' is no longer acting – you suddenly realise you are doing it. Let's say you want to make a positive impact on your boss and get the promotion you are after: start to act like someone who holds the position you want.

Programme your mind to have confidence

You can programme your mind to have confidence with various simple but effective techniques.

● **Create a picture of confidence**: See yourself how you would like to be, as if you already have the impact you would like to have, in situations where you would like to have it.

Maybe you have got some old mental movies that sap your energy. You think about going for an interview and immediately the memory pops up into your mind of the last one you went to. Did that ever go bad! You do not want that to happen again. So you – perhaps unconsciously – decide not to apply.

You need to zap that memory. Bring the picture up in your mind and start to change its qualities. If it is a movie, make it into a still picture, move it away, make it smaller, turn down the soundtrack; then when you look at it or listen to it again, you don't feel bad. Learn what you need from it, then let it go.

Exercise

Think of the last few times you were in the limelight. Focus on what went well. Now imagine you are a film director with you also playing the part of someone who is confident. Run the movie several times, adjusting it until you are entirely happy with the result. Now step into the 'you' on the screen and play the scene again – this time looking out through your own eyes. If you are not quite content with the result, cycle round again until it feels exactly right. Now think of a future time when you want to feel really confident. Check how you feel about it now. If it feels okay, you are done; if not, repeat the process above until you feel confident enough to say 'Bring it on'.

- **Zap that critical inner voice:** We all have an inner critic: a voice inside our heads that will let us know when we are not up to scratch. The voice has a positive intention to protect us from making or repeating mistakes, taking risks or looking foolish. It can drive you to reach higher standards. 'If I work harder I can make it to the top.' It stops you from being hurt or feeling rejected. By predicting a possible negative outcome you can prepare yourself for the worst. But when you feel guilty the critic provides lashings of punishment – beating you up with words and feelings.

Exercise

Has it ever occurred to you that you can change your inner voice? It is yours – it is part of you – so why not? Where is it located in your mind's eye? What happens if you move it somewhere else? What is the tone? Why not give it a different quality, perhaps with the voice purring like a cat? Or how about turning your critic into a coach that champions you when the going gets tough, saying 'You are the best' instead of 'You are so rubbish'. There is a great little book entitled *What to Say When You Talk to Yourself*, by Shad Helmstetter, which is full of great ideas for making powerful changes like these.

- **Manage your state**: If you have a tendency to get anxious during a meeting or networking event, you need to find ways of managing your state and keeping your emotions under control. You can remain cool, calm and collected by breathing deeply, expecting a positive outcome, and remembering that you have as much right to offer your opinions as anyone else.

 Exercise

Remember a time when you felt confident. Replay the movie of that memory in your mind. Make the colours more vivid, add a soundtrack, adjust the volume until it sounds just right for you. Get in touch with that feeling of confidence; notice where in your body you feel it. Imagine that you have a remote control with a button for controlling that feeling. Turn it up. Then some more. Keep going until it feels fantastic. As it reaches its peak, squeeze your thumb and little finger together on your left hand.

Whenever you want to feel that way again, squeeze your thumb and little finger together. Your unconscious mind will be obliged to replay that feeling whenever you need it.

If you find it hard to use one of your senses, do not worry: we all have one or two senses that are stronger than the others. The exercise will still work.

Prepare, prepare, prepare

As with many things in life, the better prepared we are the more confident we feel.

Before going to a meeting, make sure you do your homework; perhaps making a few brief notes you can refer to during the meeting, should your mind suddenly go blank. Prepare a list of points you want to raise or questions you want to ask.

If you are planning to attend a networking event, scour the papers and listen to the news for a few days beforehand. Make sure you are up to speed with the latest TV programmes. In short, be ready with your small talk. If the event is centred around a particular topic, prepare yourself to be able to talk about that too.

If at an event you find yourself among a group who are talking about a topic you don't understand, ask them questions to find out more about it. People love to talk about things they find interesting and will be only too delighted to have a new audience. If you are really not interested in the minutiae of a technical aspect of some complex auditing principles, politely move on saying, 'Hey, this is way over my head guys, I'll see you later.'

Assert yourself with confidence

How do you react when:

- you have been waiting for a long time in a queue and someone pushes in front of you

- a colleague chats noisily when you are trying to concentrate

- your boss asks you to work late again – and you are going out

- someone asks you for help but you are busy

- you have been promised some figures but they have not been sent and you need them urgently

- your boss takes credit for something you have done

- an acquaintance constantly puts you down in front of friends

- you have lent someone some money and they have not paid it back or, a host of other occasions when you are called upon to be assertive? Do you say what you think, want and feel, or are you tentative, uncomfortable and accommodating?

 Case study: Nelson Mandela

A quiet unassuming man, Nelson Mandela became a symbol of freedom and equality around the world. When he was released from prison after 27 years (most of which were spent in Robben Island) on 11 February 1990, he continued to spearhead the fight against apartheid in South Africa. His approach was one of reconciliation and negotiation. In 1993 he was awarded the Nobel Peace Prize – one of many awards. Admired by many, this inspirational statesman is not loud, not extrovert, not brash; rather he is quietly spoken, determined and seemingly endlessly patient. 'Let's give up' is not in his vocabulary. He demonstrates how it is possible to make a massive impact on the lives of many people without all the usual 'rah-rah'.

Being assertive creates impact

Assertiveness is central to personal impact. When you hold back, put others first all the time and do not stand your ground, you come across as a weak and indecisive 'people pleaser' – a doormat they can walk all over. How much personal impact can you have when others see you like that?

It is a similar, but different, story when you are too assertive – just going after what you want without worrying about anyone else. This is aggression – and it can be every bit as damaging to your impact. You may be experienced as a bully who is insensitive and uncaring.

Understanding assertion, aggression and non-assertion

Being clear about the differences between assertion, aggression and non-assertion is the first step to choosing assertion more often. The descriptions below clarify each type of behaviour.

Assertion

People who behave assertively stand up for their rights in a way that does not violate other people's rights. They express their needs, wants, opinions, feelings and beliefs in direct, honest and appropriate ways. They also believe what they say is worth listening to.

Aggression

Some people confuse assertion with aggressive behaviour, which is quite different and creates a negative impact. Someone who stands up for their rights in a way that does not respect the rights of others is behaving aggressively. They may ignore or dismiss other people's needs, wants, opinions, feelings and beliefs. They often put forward their views in a way that upsets others.

Submission

Equally, if you do not stand up for your rights, or do so in a way that means others can easily disregard them, you will not be effective. People who behave in a submissive manner often come across in apologetic, diffident or self-effacing ways. This greatly reduces their impact.

(With thanks to Back and Back, *Assertiveness at Work*)

What stops you being assertive?

What stops people who behave submissively from being assertive – and maximising their impact – is often concern about how others might react. They worry they will not be liked – that saying what they want or arguing their case might jeopardise the relationship, and they will be rejected. Sometimes they are sensitive to other people's feelings and, because they would hate to be thought of as aggressive, they over-compensate and end up appearing submissive.

The reverse is true for many of those who act in an aggressive manner. They do not want to appear weak, so they put on a show of strength to make sure it does not happen. Once again, this backfires and a negative impression is conveyed.

10 top tips to assertively having more impact

1   **Making requests**: Make requests in an open and straightforward way rather than trying to make it difficult for the other person to refuse. Do not apologise (for example, 'I'm sorry to trouble you...'), be direct and brief (for example, 'I'd like the report by the end of the week'). Give a reason for your request but do not use flattery or play on their good nature. Respect their right to say 'no' and don't take a refusal personally.

2   **Refusing requests**: Keep your reply brief, but not abrupt, rather than a long rambling explanation. Use a warm voice tone. Acknowledge the person who has made the request and give the real reason for saying 'no'. Ask for more time or greater clarity about their request (for example, 'Do you need it by the end of the week?'). If they persist in requesting, repeat your refusal.

3   **Disagreeing and stating your views**: Clearly state the reasons why you disagree and express any doubts you have in a constructive way (for example, 'I see your difficulty. Can we get round it?'). Recognise and acknowledge the other person's view and state which parts you agree with. Be prepared to change your opinion in the light of new information.

4   **Giving praise**: Maintain eye contact and make it specific, clear and brief (for example, 'I like the way you handled the team meeting and managed to keep to time').

5   **Giving negative feedback**: Be honest, objective and sensitive. It is about the behaviour not the person. As with giving praise, maintain eye contact and make it specific, clear and brief (for example, 'I think you will chair the team meeting more effectively if you keep to time').

▶

6 **Receiving praise**: Thank the praise-giver briefly (for example, 'Thanks, Amanda, I'm glad you liked it'). Agree with or accept the praise. If you like something, it is assertive to say so (for example, 'Thank you, Jatinder, I was pleased with the report'). If you disagree, thank them and qualify your response.

7 **Receiving negative feedback**: Listen carefully to what the feedback-giver has to say. Ask for more information if you are unclear. Ask what it was specifically they were unhappy with. If the criticism is valid, agree and apologise, if this is appropriate. If it is not, disagree and state your view positively.

8 **Giving bad news**: Take the initiative and state what has happened clearly. Explain the actions, if any, that you propose to take. Keep it brief and factual. Maintain eye contact and indicate any implications there are for the person. Listen to their suggestions for dealing with the problem or situation.

9 **Being proactive and positive**: Take the initiative, make things happen.

10 **Using assertive language**: This makes a big difference to the impact you make. Rather than 'Can I offer an idea? It might not be much good but...', say, in a confident tone with strong body language, 'My idea is ...'

Just say 'no'

Some people find 'no' to be one of the hardest words to say. They feel that by refusing a request they will be judged as uncooperative, unhelpful, selfish and uncaring. If that is you, try the following steps.

- **Keep the reply short**: Simply say 'no' and recognise you do not have to justify your decision or make excuses. Avoid lengthy explanations which the other person can challenge or debate.

- **Acknowledge the response**: Recognise the person's feelings and avoid becoming emotionally involved (for example, the reply to 'I think you are being very selfish' might be 'Yes, I can see how you might think that, but my answer is still no').

- **Use repetition**. Most people give in too easily when they want to say 'no'. Many of us are simply too nice and not persistent enough. You might feel you're not getting through and your refusal has not been acknowledged. Find a form of words which succinctly expresses your wishes and keep repeating them until the other person realises you mean what you say.

- **Self-disclose**: Be honest about your feelings at that exact moment: (for example, 'I feel awkward when I have to refuse ...', 'I feel uneasy when you raise your voice'. Be sure to use 'I' messages and avoid accusing (for example, not 'You make me feel ...')

- **Show empathy**: Express how you feel towards the other person. This is particularly important if you are using repetition (for example, 'I understand how difficult it is and how over-worked you are at present, but my answer is still no').

- **Workable compromise**: Seek an alternative solution to the problem by meeting the other person halfway without losing your self-esteem (for example, 'I can't stay late, but I could come in earlier tomorrow if that will help').

- **Maintain rapport**: Remember throughout the exchange your body language should support your words. Use direct eye contact, vocal energy and open posture to state your views assertively.

Impact comes in 'cans'

Tom believed he would never succeed – and, funnily enough, he didn't. Bob believed he would and – surprise, surprise – he did. There is a wonderful quote from Henry Ford, founder of the Ford Motor Company: 'Believe you can, believe you can't: either way you are right.'

Expectation creates experience. What we think will happen tends to happen – because at an unconscious level we mobilise all our resources to *make it happen*. We prove ourselves right. That is why it is important to know what you want and then believe you can achieve it. You are creating a self-fulfilling prophecy.

If you believe you will make a positive impact at an important meeting, you will behave in a way that ensures you do. If you worry your presentation will go wrong, you will be anxious and it will. Mindset is everything when it comes to making an impact. People who have a can-do attitude go out into the world and make things happen. They act with confidence. They are assertive. Impact comes in 'cans'.

Many of us, though, live in a world where there are too many 'can'ts': 'I can't ask my boss for a raise', 'I can't chair that meeting', 'I can't talk to strangers'. Can't is a four-letter word – and a nasty one at that. It holds you back. It stops you trying – and it stops you succeeding. Beliefs can be a powerful driving force in helping you achieve the impact you want – but they can also hold you back.

 Case study: Jane Tomlinson

'Had Jane Tomlinson been granted a long and healthy life, it is unlikely that she would have become known beyond her home town of Rothwell, near Leeds. But she became extraordinary – and famous – when, in 2002, she ran the London Marathon and raised money for charity while suffering from terminal cancer.'

So begins the obituary for Jane Tomlinson in *The Times*. An inspiration for millions of people, and an individual with enormous personal impact, she achieved more while battling with cancer than many of us do in good health. Her example shows that no matter who you are, no matter what your background is, or your present situation, you can make an impact on others.

Limiting beliefs and empowering beliefs

A good way to identify your beliefs is to catch yourself saying 'I can' or 'I can't'. Whenever you use the word 'can't' you need to challenge yourself. Is it really true? Sometimes beliefs are simply illogical or irrational. Dispute beliefs that are not working for you with 'What if I could?', or 'What would happen if I did?' Listen out as well for expressions such as 'must' or 'musn't,' or 'should' or 'shouldn't' – they all represent powerful beliefs that shape your potential for personal impact.

But who put all those ideas, beliefs, and thoughts in your mind? Not you, that's for sure. They came from your parents, your teachers, your siblings – from experiences you had when you were younger. Is that it, then, you are stuck with them for life? Of course not. Beliefs are not fixed – you can change them. In fact, they naturally evolve over time. Think of a belief you used to have which you no longer hold to be true. Do you still believe in Father Christmas? Sorry to disappoint you, but it was your parents who left those presents under the tree. Perhaps there was a time when you never believed you would be able to do something and then you went and did it. Maybe you spent years being completely unfit and after six months of training completed the London Marathon.

 Exercise

Stop and think for a moment about some of the beliefs you hold about yourself – particularly in relation to the word 'can't'. Which ones serve you? Which stop you from making a positive impact?

The power of negative thinking

There is a lot of talk about the power of positive thinking – but what about the power of negative thinking? 'You can't light a fire', sang Bruce Springsteen in 'Dancing in the Dark', 'worrying about your little world falling apart'. It can be hard to stay positive when the going gets tough.

Sometimes you will experience a setback or two. Things do not always go the way you hope. The secret then is to find a way to move to 'cause' rather than being stuck at 'effect'.

When you start out in a new role or step up to a new challenge it is natural to feel uncertain about your ability to cope. After just a few weeks or months of actually doing it, you realise you can not only manage it but do it well.

The more positive experiences you have in various areas of your life, the more self-belief you will have. When you say to yourself, 'Bring it on, I can do it', your self-belief comes across in the way you express your ideas, your body posture, the way you move and your voice tone. Because you believe in yourself, other people believe that what you have to say is worth listening to. This forms a virtuous circle of reinforcement.

Design the impact you want

All things are created twice. The blueprint comes first, then the building. The menu, then the meal. Look inside your mind – what are you creating in there?

We have given you lots to think about and many ideas to apply. Our advice is to revisit this chapter over the coming weeks and apply the ideas to different situations you come across. If this seems hard to do on your own, talk to others to boost your morale – friends, family, colleagues, or get a coach.

Above all, believe in yourself – no matter what others might say. Develop a positive mental attitude and your confidence and assertiveness will increase. Any 'failure' you have is simply useful feedback for being even better next time. Once you have applied the techniques in this chapter there will be no holding you back. Like Lewis Hamilton, you will be speeding along in the driving seat of your life, creating a positive impact wherever you go.

In the words of those famous American philosophers, Nike – *just do it!*

Make an impact now

● Identify the beliefs that get in the way of you being all you can be.

● Practise moving with a feeling of ease – acting as if you have all the confidence you need.

● Work out where you most want to make an impact and go for it – have total self-belief that you can achieve it.

Chapter 2
The brand called 'You'

'*A brand is a promise.*'

Walter Landor, branding pioneer

You are wandering around an unfamiliar city and you fancy a coffee. You check out the options. There are a few local coffee shops along with some well-known chains, including Starbucks and Costa. Which do you go for? Or you want something to eat. Subway? McDonald's? Pizza Hut? Or a restaurant whose name you do not recognise?

For most people it is a no-brainer. They go for a brand they know, like and trust. There is no way of telling how good the places are they have not been to before. If they have had a positive experience somewhere in the past, they tend to go back.

You go shopping for a laptop. Two models with an identical specification catch your eye. The Sony costs 20 per cent more than the other brand which you do not recognise, but you decide it is worth paying the extra to be sure of getting a computer you can rely on.

'Give me a Bud'

We live in a branded world. We do not ask for beer, we ask for Stella or Bud. We do not buy clothes and accessories, we choose Gap, Moschino, Diesel or Versace. Most of us like some brands and dislike others. We may even identify with certain names and buy them exclusively – always shopping in the same store or driving the same make of car.

The world's leading businesses recognise the importance of brands and branding. Some are obsessed by it. In her book *No Logo*, Naomi Klein argues that some international companies now consider the creation and marketing of their brand to be more important than the product or service they offer. Most have a multitude of marketing experts whose responsibility it is to manage the perception of the brand. They do not leave it to chance – there is too much at stake.

What is a brand? Think of Nike. Is it the name? No. It's not the logo either – the swoosh that is known throughout the world. It's not even the various products – trainers, clothing, etc. – on which the name and logo appear. It is more subtle than that.

A brand, in the words of Walter Landor, is a *promise*. It is a promise of what you can expect when you buy it, use it and experience it. That promise can often be expressed in a simple phrase or even a single word. What comes to mind when you think of Volvo? Safety. How about BMW? The ultimate driving machine. Rolls-Royce? Luxury.

Brands seek to differentiate themselves from their competitors. If your product is the same as all the others in your category or sector, why would anyone choose it in preference to what else is available? You need to make it stand out from the crowd – to give it a recognisable face.

But the most important thing to understand is the powerful emotional pull brands exert. People seek them out. They know what they are getting and feel good when they use them. They are loyal to them. Which means consumers will pay over the odds for their preferred brand.

Put a Nike swoosh on a T-shirt and its value increases by at least a factor of five. A restaurant with a Michelin star or two commands prices well in excess of your average eatery. Almost all premium products cost more than rival offerings. Which is why companies invest so much time, money and effort into building strong brands.

People can be brands, too

This is all very interesting, you may be saying to yourself, but what has it got to do with impact? Which is a fair question to ask. The answer is simple: *people can be brands, too.*

This is an approach that many celebrities are now taking – from the movies to sport to music to television – they think of themselves as brands, and package and present themselves as if they were products. Some even copyright their own image to prevent others using it without permission.

Gene Simmons, who fronts the rock band Kiss, once said that while he liked being in a rock and roll band, he loved being in a rock and roll *brand.* That is certainly what they are: they have their own logo, their own distinctive make-up and a stage show that is larger than life. The point he was making was that brands typically earn a lot more than bands. There is a world of difference. People will pay top dollar to see a band or performer with a strong, commanding brand.

The same is true of you. When your brand is clear and powerful, you will increase your earning potential because others will recognise more clearly the value you add.

Why would anyone want to buy you?

What exactly is a personal brand? How does it differ from corporate branding? Peter Montoya, the author of *The Personal Branding Phenomenon*, describes a personal brand as 'A personal identity that stimulates precise, meaningful perceptions in its audience of the qualities and values that person stands for'.

Personal branding is about taking a strategic marketing approach to the impression you create and the impact you make. Too many people leave it to chance; when they interact with others they have no real idea how they want to be perceived. As a result they end up sending mixed or confused messages.

In an interview you need to stand out. At a networking event you need to be able to communicate what sets you apart. In a meeting you need to come across as someone with a contribution. Many people cannot read between the lines, so you have to be able to communicate, clearly and consistently, what makes you different – what makes you special. Think of yourself as a product or service, and ask yourself 'Why would anyone want to buy me?' This forces you to focus on the essence of who you are and what you have to offer. Then it is simply a matter of ensuring that what you do, how you do it, and what you say and how you say it, creates an impression that aligns with your brand.

Here are the most obvious ways in which people are branded:

- personality
- ability
- profession/job
- achievements
- lifestyle
- friends
- appearance
- interests/hobbies/pastimes
- possessions
- behaviours/actions.

 Exercise

Jot down a few notes on anything that people associate with you, using this branding list. Maybe you are famous for changing the colour of your hair every few months, being football-mad or as a dedicated nurse, teacher, accountant, etc.

Does your list match the image you want to portray? Does it add to your impact or reduce it?

Isn't personal branding all smoke and mirrors?

Now some of you may be thinking, 'Hold on – isn't all this personal branding business just one big con?' You pretend to be something you are not in order to get what you want. Is it just all smoke and mirrors? You are faking it. Putting on a mask. Playing a role.

You could easily see it like that, but that is not what we are suggesting. As Mary Spillane says in the highly readable *Branding Yourself*, 'a successful brand must be true to itself'. You cannot just invent an image that just is not you; that will not work. You need to be able to deliver on the promise of your brand. Which means there must be a match between what you say you are and how you are seen by others. Personal branding isn't only about changing what you wear or having your hair done differently.

> you need to be able to deliver on the promise of your brand

You have probably had the experience of trying a product or service and finding it is not what it was cracked up to be. If the reality doesn't live up to the promise, you never buy it again. It is the same with personal branding. There is no point in putting up a persona that people will see through, or creating a completely different identity that those who know you do not recognise.

Do you want to live someone else's life? What would that be like? You would be constantly worrying about being 'found out'. If you simply take a 'smoke and mirrors' approach you will soon come unstuck. Your starting point needs to be what is important to you – your values, your beliefs, your vision. You need to be who you really are as a brand.

Getting started on your brand

Before you think about what people might say about you, how would you describe yourself at your very best? Reliable, loyal, ambitious, caring, eccentric, fun, creative…? What is it you would like colleagues to say about you if you were leaving the company? Or friends and family in a special birthday celebration speech?

We all have a set of guiding principles or beliefs that act like a compass. They represent what is most important to us – our values – and we use them to tell us whether something is right or wrong, good or bad. David McNally and Karl Speak, authors of *Be Your Own Brand*, describe a brand as 'A special type of relationship – one that involves the kind of trust that only happens when two people believe there is a direct connection between their value systems'. Being aware of your values is not only about how you want to be perceived by others, it also gives you clarity and focus over how you want to live your life. In fact, you do not have to try; it just happens. If you value friendliness you will go out of your way to be friendly to people, and you will soon win a reputation as a friendly person.

 Exercise

The table below contains a list of common values. Compare this with some of the words you thought of earlier that describe you. Are there any you would like to add to your list?

Acceptance	Appreciation	Commitment	Cooperation
Accountability	Authenticity	Community	Courage
Accuracy	Autonomy	Compassion	Creativity
Achievement	Balance	Competition	Curiosity
Acknowledgement	Boldness	Comradeship	Democracy
Adaptability	Calmness	Contribution	Dependability
Adventure	Collaboration	Control	Detachment

Determination	Harmony	Modesty	Safety
Directness	Health	Morality	Self-awareness
Discipline	Helpfulness	Obedience	Self-reliance
Economic security	Honesty	Openness	Self-respect
Education	Honour	Optimism	Sensitivity
Effort	Humility	Order	Sharing
Elegance	Humour	Organisation	Sincerity
Empathy	Imagination	Patience	Spirituality
Empowerment	Independence	Partnership	Stability
Enthusiasm	Individualism	Peace	Success
Equality	Influence	Perfection	Tact
Excellence	Integrity	Perseverance	Tenacity
Fairness	Intuition	Personal	Thoughtfulness
Family	Joy	development	Tolerance
Focus	Justice	Pleasure	Tradition
Forgiveness	Kindness	Power	Trust
Freedom	Learning	Prudence	Truthfulness
Friendliness	Levity	Quality	Understanding
Fun	Love	Recognition	Variety
Generosity	Loyalty	Respect	Vitality
Gentleness	Mercy	Responsibility	Wealth
Happiness	Moderation	Risk-taking	Wisdom

Once you have created a list, ask yourself this question: 'If I could only have one, which would it be?' Whatever you come up with is your number-one value. Let us imagine the word you chose was freedom. Now ask yourself, 'If I could only have freedom and one other, which would it be?' Keep going until you have a list of five to ten values.

Next to each value write a short description. For example: 'Freedom – being able to make my own decisions and explore new opportunities.'

Two people with the same value may describe it in a completely different way. Our values are what make us unique. We form our sense of identity from our values.

Walking the talk

It is one thing being clear about what is important to you and quite another living up to that ideal. People will only trust your brand promise if you walk the talk. Being aware of your values allows you to monitor how well you are living up to your own expectations. The clothes you wear, the work you do, the way you are in the world need to be aligned to who you are. When you are real, your actions match your words. You are not afraid to be yourself. When you let people experience the real you, you connect with them and they trust you.

What is your brand right now?

But you are not, of course, starting from scratch. You already have a personal brand. Everyone you meet forms an impression of you, whether you like it or not – and whether you deliberately set out to shape it or not.

So one of the first things you need to establish is what your brand is right now. There is no point in revamping your personal identity only to find it is totally different from what others think of you right now. You might get away with that if you are a celebrity (it is not unusual for them to have a periodic makeover), but if you are just an average Joe or Josephine, others may be confused – shocked even – if you suddenly start to act or talk in an unfamiliar way.

The starting point for creating your personal brand is self-awareness. Take a good look at yourself and be prepared to acknowledge your weaknesses as well as your strengths.

 Exercice

What gets in the way? What do you want to change? If you are not sure, ask half a dozen people who know you well for some feedback on what they like about you and what drives them crazy. Do they see you as warm and friendly or grumpy and miserable? Are you someone who is reliable, who always gets things done on time, or do they think you procrastinate, or let others down? Ask lots of open questions, and listen carefully to the answers. You will find out whether you are living your values.

Understanding how others perceive you will provide you with useful insights into the brand you have already created. Having established where you are now, you can start to consider what you want to change in order to improve your personal impact.

Completing this exercise will give you some idea of your personal brand as it stands at the moment, but there is one problem: most people are nice, and they may not tell you the truth. Or the whole truth, at least. If they like you or love you they may sugar-coat the negatives – while some people find it hard to dish out praise. You may have to coax and cajole them to get the truth.

Another option is to reflect on things people have said to you spontaneously. 'You are such a supportive friend', 'That presentation seemed rather disorganised', 'We always know you will do a good job'. What do you hear time and again? Any comments that various people have voiced in different contexts are likely to be representative of how others experience you. You may be different at work from the way you are with family or friends. 'I'm a hard-hitting, just-do-it trouble-shooter at work, an adoring husband and loving father, and a competitive but social tennis player.'

One option is to enrol on a personal impact course. There, in a safe, supportive, small-group environment, you can get honest, constructive feedback on the impression you make – along with advice on how to improve anything that is not working for you.

A 'brand' new you?

The essence of branding is differentiation. What is your USP – your unique self-proposition? You need to be distinctive, so people know what is you and what is not you. Why *would* anyone want to buy you? Having bought you once, why would they buy you *again and again*? If you do not have anything of value, nobody is likely to care about your brand anyway. It is obvious, but true nonetheless. The aim is to build 'brand loyalty', so that given a choice people will go for your brand in preference to others that are available. To do that you need to create the perception that your 'product' is unique.

Your brand also needs to stand for something. Ideally you should 'own' a word, or an idea. Nike is about winning. Harley Davidson is about freedom. What is the essence of you? Your answer to that question needs to be focused and clear. You cannot be all things to all men and all women. Your number-one value is likely to lie at the heart of your brand.

 Exercise

1   What skills, knowledge and experience do you have? Take a blank sheet of paper and list as many things as possible.

2   Ask yourself, 'What do I do that I'm proud of? How do I add value?' Note down the answers.

3   Create a description of you as if you were a product or service (for example, 'Amy is reliable, trustworthy and fun to do business with. When she encounters a problem she perseveres until she has found a solution that works').

4   Define your USP – your unique self-proposition (for example, 'I help people solve problems').

Getting your message out there

Once you have defined your brand and created it, you need to market it effectively. We are talking advertising, PR, and all the tricks that organisations use to communicate their messages. You need to create a coherent development programme for your brand. What does that mean in practice for an individual without millions of pounds or dollars to spend?

One simple but effective way is to enhance your visibility:

- **Get out there**: Get yourself known by attending networking events or company conferences. Volunteer to do things that will raise your profile.

- **Be alert for opportunities**: Be proactive and consider what kind of opportunities may arise that you can take advantage of, such as a secondment to another department or getting involved with an exciting, high-profile project to help your local community.

- **Take chances when they come**: An opportunity to raise your visibility may appear out of the blue. Someone may interview you for the company magazine or you get the chance to fill in for your boss at a meeting.

Here are a few more ideas to get you started:

- Offer to chair meetings or lead discussions whenever the opportunity arises.

- Volunteer to get involved in a project – even better, make it outside your current area of responsibility.

- Get acknowledged as an expert by delivering a presentation on your special subject – or even offer to run a training course, if appropriate.

- Write a piece for the company newsletter or magazine and submit it to the editor. They are always looking for something interesting to fill the space.

- Attend internal and external networking/social events – become a familiar face on the circuit.

Whatever you decide to do, make it a campaign. Sustain it. One article in the newsletter is not going to be enough on its own. You cannot make an effort for one month and then just stop. It can take time to build a strong, enduring personal brand.

Living your brand consistently

You go into a McDonald's in London, St Petersburg or Tokyo and it is an identical experience, give or take some relatively minor local differences. It is the same with every major brand. If consistency is crucial with products and services, it is critical with personal branding.

We only trust brands when they are consistent. If you only receive good service in a store sometimes, you won't feel confident. Inconsistency destroys trust, so you need to be reliable. Brands are strengthened by repetition. Every time you are exposed to a brand and it delivers on its promise, you trust it more.

Some people are changeable. Mercurial. One minute they are up, the next they are down. This time they are warm and compassionate, next time they are harsh and critical. You never know where you are with them. They do not have a consistent brand, and that is a problem. Everything you do should be consistent, aligned and congruent.

Being consistent is, of course, easier said than done. We are all subject to moods and sometimes behave in different ways from one situation to another, but it is crucial that you seek to be as consistent as possible in your dealings with others. Branding, even when it comes to people, is *always* a promise. It is an indication of how you will act in any given situation.

Madonna, David Bowie ... and you

You might be tempted to think that once you have branded yourself that is it – job done. But it isn't like that. Madonna has reinvented herself many times. So has David Bowie. So have many other celebrities. So should you. Times change. You change. Which means your brand image needs to change. From time to time you need to give yourself a makeover to reflect where you are in your life.

The secret is to audit your brand periodically, reviewing and revising it as necessary. Go back to people you asked to give you feedback last time and ask them again. Has their impression of you changed? Check in with people who have come into your life. How do they experience you? Is your personal brand still aligned with who you are and creating the impression you want? If it isn't, continue to make whatever adjustments are necessary. Branding and rebranding is never done.

You are the CEO of 'Me plc'

If you want to increase your impact you need to stop thinking of yourself as just a person and instead appoint yourself CEO of 'Me plc'. Review and revise your personal brand in line with your values. Then get out there and show them what you've got!

Make an impact now

● Make a first stab at defining your USP (unique self-proposition) *now*.

● Ask three people today to give you honest feedback on how you come across.

● Come up with one way in which you can raise your profile and take action immediately.

Chapter 3

Make a positive first impression in seven seconds

'You never get a second chance to make a first impression.'

Anon

Some say it is 30 seconds; others say ten, seven or three. Psychologists Janine Willis and Alexander Todorov found it can even be a tenth of a second. But let us not get hung up on *exactly* how long it is – that doesn't really matter – what is important is that you realise how little time you have to make a positive first impression. A tenth of a second perhaps overstates it, we reckon you have probably got no more than seven seconds.

When anyone meets you anywhere they size you up, they evaluate you, they judge you – and within seconds they have pretty much made their mind up about you. It takes about as long as it took you to read that last sentence. Research shows that first impressions are lasting impressions – the opinions others form of us right at the start of a relationship rarely change. One study suggests it takes at least eight pieces of positive information to overcome a negative first impression. So if you get off to a bad start, you may find it a challenge to recover from it.

Scary, isn't it? Your success in a wide range of situations, from dates to job interviews, from selling to networking, rests to a large degree on your ability to make a positive first impression – and you have an incredibly narrow window of opportunity. That means you cannot afford to leave anything to chance. You need to plan carefully to create precisely the impression you want.

Harnessing the halo effect ...

Alex meets Jo and soon observes that she is quick-witted. Because he values this characteristic he unconsciously credits her with several other characteristics, such as being intelligent, creative and articulate. He does not base this on any evidence, or any judgement – she may or may not have these qualities – it is just an association in his mind. This is known as the halo effect. It is something we all do and it's extremely powerful.

 Exercise

Pause for a moment and think: what traits or behaviours do you consider important in others? When you meet someone with them, do you 'give them a halo', and start to see other traits and behaviours which they may not have?

Since many people share the same preferences – kindness, intelligence and a sense of humour to name but three – you can harness the halo effect to increase your personal impact. All you have to do is demonstrate those behaviours when you are with others. You will not be successful every time, but you should have a good strike rate.

Each person will, of course, have their own, individual bias which you won't know about – cannot know about – initially at least. But over time, as you get to know people, you will become more aware of their preferences and will be able to adapt and adjust your behaviour accordingly. The more you can show aspects of your personality in those first few moments that others value, the more you will benefit from the halo effect as they 'give' you several other favourable qualities and end up thinking you are great.

... and watching out for the horns

More important than the halo effect, at least when it comes to impact, is the horns effect. It works in the same way, except the trait in question is one that people dislike.

Take scruffy, unpolished shoes. It's no big deal – right? Who cares whether you give them a shine or not? Well, actually, a lot of people care – and they care a lot. Because of the horns effect, they may end up thinking you are lazy, 'downmarket' or lack attention to detail – all because of scruffy, unpolished shoes.

Or how about being late for a meeting? Does it really matter? Just a few minutes? Yes, it does – it *really* does. Many, many, many people will mark you down for it. On account of the horns effect, they may also consider you disrespectful, unprofessional and disorganised.

This process of taking one thing you don't like about a person and extending it without evidence and by assumption to other attributes is, of course, how stereotyping and prejudice works. It is not just about colour, race, gender, culture, age, religion or sexual preference, it can be height, size, facial hair, wearing a particular item of clothing, or using a knife incorrectly.

We make connections between characteristics or behaviours we don't like and then sort for more evidence to confirm the stereotype. It is not deliberate, it happens out of conscious awareness.

As with the halo effect, there will be individual preferences, but many common themes – ranging from spelling mistakes in emails, to not standing up when someone approaches you, to having a weak handshake. So, once again, it makes good sense to minimise behaviours that may invoke the horns effect if you want to maximise your impact when you first meet someone.

Shape their perception of you ahead of time

When you know you are going to meet someone – it is not just a chance encounter – there are actions you can take ahead of time to shape their opinion of you. If you do not, they will form an impression from what they know already. In the business world you may be judged by your perceived status, the job you do, or on what people have read about you. In an interview this could be your CV, in a meeting it might be an email you have sent. In a social setting people start to create an opinion of you from what they know about your interests and the 'crowd' you hang around with. Once you are aware of how your reputation goes before you it is possible to plan ahead. Where you can, shape what others say about you. Play on your strengths in written communication without bragging or boasting, and minimise any potential weaknesses by focusing on your strong points.

Impressions at a distance

As you stroll down a street, walk into a wine bar, step on to a train or enter a crowded room, people become aware of your presence. Some may glance your way, others will catch a glimpse of you out of the corner of their eye. You have no relationship with any of them yet, but they have started to form a view about you.

What is that first impression built on? Only things that can be observed from a distance: your clothing, accessories and hairstyle, the way you stand and move. They will not see the finer details but they will notice anything that stands out. Since we are talking about the impact you have before you even meet, it is primarily visual information they will use. Depending on the situation, they may sometimes hear you laugh. We will be discussing how to make the most of your vocal impact in Chapter 8, but for now the focus is on what people see and the impact this makes on them in those first few moments.

People often 'judge a book by its cover'

From five metres away the colour of the cloth and the style of your clothes start to reveal things about you. People will notice immediately if you are dressed in beige when dark tones are the norm. They will also spot any obvious colour clashes – 'blue and green should never be seen' – and mark you down for it. In most people's eyes, what you wear makes a statement about who you are.

Here are four ways to make a positive impact through the way you dress:

1 **Dress for the occasion**: The most important thing is to get the level right. Black tie? Smart? Smart casual? Casual? Get it wrong and you can stand out like a sore thumb – and end up feeling uncomfortable. Putting on a bright tie or dramatic scarf when everyone else has dressed down – they are in T-shirts and trainers – can be as bad as under-dressing. Our advice is to match what you think others might choose. If in doubt, go one step above. It is easy to remove a tie or jacket to create a relaxed look in a moment.

   Some people worry about what to wear for important social or business occasions. The obvious solution is to ask the organiser about the dress code, or the host if it is a social gathering. It is not always that simple though. If you are attending an interview, visiting a customer for the first time, or going on a blind date, you have to use your judgement.

2 **Don't flash too much flesh**: This goes for men as much as women. There are times – a relaxed barbeque, a pool party – when skimpy clothing may be okay, but take care in business situations. Women who wear skirts that look like belts or have a plunging neckline will make plenty of impact – but is it the impact they want to make? Men, too, need to watch what they are doing when ties come off. By all means undo a couple of buttons, but three or four can be too much, and send the

wrong kind of signal. It is the same with rolling up shirt sleeves: in a professional setting it can sometimes be a no-no.

3   **Go for a good cut and style**: Even from a distance people notice when your suit is well cut, or your jeans do you justice. Invest in one or two stylish, quality pieces that are well made, for occasions that are especially important. Casual wear needs some thought and attention, too. Buy the best your budget will allow: one well-made item is worth three from bargain-basement stores where clothes are often made down to price rather than up to standard.

4   **Review your wardrobe**: Take a tip from Trinny and Susannah, authors of bestselling books such as *What Not to Wear*, and go through your wardrobe item by item. Make sure your clothes fit well, are in good condition and are up to date.

Ask someone you trust to give you honest feedback, or challenge yourself. Does this fit properly? This is not simply a matter of taste; if you have to breathe in to do the zip up, it will look unsightly and reduce your impact. If you look in the mirror and see bulges in all the wrong places, you need to chuck it out – even if it is one of your favourite outfits.

Don't get stuck in a time warp. You need to give your wardrobe a new lease of life. If most of the items in your wardrobe are more than five years old, it is time for some retail therapy.

Not sure what to buy? Read a couple of magazines appropriate to your age and sex to get an idea of what would work best for you. If not, ask a sales assistant or savvy friend for advice. Think about your unique self-proposition (see Chapter 2) and go for items that fit the image you want to create. If you have not worn an item in the last two years, it is time to say goodbye. Take it to a charity shop.

What about clothes you love which have seen better days? Wear them around the house or put them in the bin. If an item is marked, torn, has gone out of shape or has buttons missing, people will notice – even across a crowded room. Get clothes repaired or throw them out. Be ruthless in purging your wardrobe: only keep clothes that make you look good.

'Are these scales right?'

Your size is one of the first things people notice about you – and some will form a negative impression when they first see you if it is at an extreme in either direction of the scale. Having a hectic lifestyle can play havoc with your eating habits, but this is a crucial area when it comes to creating the impact you want. A starting point is to focus on feeling comfortable with yourself and aiming to look healthy. Ultimately, to ensure a positive first – and lasting impression – you need a focused fitness regime based around a healthy diet and an active lifestyle.

Get your personal presence oozing

When you enter a room you want people to turn, look your way, and sense something special – a presence. As we discussed in Chapter 2, it is all about attitude: the way you feel about yourself, the way you carry yourself. Alpha males and the alpha females tend to move with grace and ease, as if they have nothing to prove. The secret to having presence lies in the word itself – you need to be present in the room. If you are distracted by a problem at work or a personal issue, and your mind is elsewhere, others will know.

Closing in on you

As you get nearer to people – about two metres away – they notice more about you. In those first few seconds they start to see the small stuff. Your suit may be smart but they spot a mark on your collar. They are aware of the brand of your T-shirt and the style of your shoes. That Italian silk woven tie you are wearing stands out and says something about you. They pick up on jewellery and other accessories – bags, rings, belts, watches and bangles. They become more conscious of the colour and style of your hair. Your personal habits become more evident.

Personal habits and grooming

Here are some things you need to consider in the two-metre zone:

- **Take care of your hair**: Wash it, brush it, have it cut professionally. The style is up to you – it can be carefully groomed or fashionably unruly – as long as it suits you and creates the impact you want. Avoid roots that reveal your natural colour or a 'do-it-yourself' colour job that does not look natural. Having split ends suggests you haven't been to a hairdresser for months. Men need to have their necks shaved – people do notice.

- **Lose unpleasant personal habits**: Do not pick your nose, let off wind or anything else like this that other people will find offensive. Yes, we know it is obvious, yet so many people do these things and they will kill your impact stone dead in a second.

- **Avoid excessive aftershave or perfume**: A little dab can make you smell nice; half a bottle is overwhelming. It will have people wanting to run a mile.

- **Be careful about facial hair**: Some people have strong feelings about beards – they feel that men are hiding behind them and as a result they do not trust those people. Others have negative associations with moustaches. There is nothing wrong with either, but they do make an impact – and it can be the opposite of what you want. If you have a beard or moustache, or are thinking about growing either, ask some close friends or colleagues for their honest opinion about how you come across.

Exercise

Reflect for a moment on people you have met for the first time recently. What details do you recall about their personal habits and grooming? What impact did they make on you? How could they have improved it? Make sure you do not make those mistakes yourself.

Be brand-aware and dress to impress

Some people will spot your Dior dress, Dolce & Gabbana handbag or Chanel suit before they even take in your face. They are brand-conscious, and will give you brownie points if you have the right labels. You can make a positive impact on some people just by virtue of a subtle logo on a jacket. Designer gear can be a double-edged sword, though. Some people think Rolex watches are signals of success, while others find them tacky and pretentious.

10 things to avoid when you are up close and personal

Some of the people who have been observing you from a distance will go on to meet you – and there is a whole lot more they will notice in the first few seconds they spend with you. Here is our list of things to avoid:

1   Body odour
2   Dirty fingernails
3   Bitten fingernails
4   Chipped nail varnish
5   Dandruff on your clothes
6   Scuffed shoes
7   Too much make-up
8   Bloodshot eyes
9   Food on your face or in your teeth
10   Facial hair on women and nose hair on men

Add accessories for extra impact

It is the added extras that turn an average outfit into something special. For men, shoes, ties, rings and cufflinks are crucial ways to add personality and flair. Women have lots of options with a huge variety of handbags, shoes, jewellery, scarves and belts. One or two well-chosen pieces can turn plain attire into an exciting ensemble. Necklaces, bracelets, rings and earrings in particular can transform your look. There is a vast array of attractive and affordable costume pieces on the market that will not break the bank.

Tattoos and piercings

Love them or hate them, tattoos and body piercings are becoming more common. They often make an individual statement about who you are. Before going under the needle, though, think about the impact you want to create. One or two small, tasteful tattoos can look fine – they may even advance your impact – but if you have lots, some people will find them a turn off. The same goes for piercings – they are pretty mainstream these days, but in some business environments a pin through your nose or tongue might create a negative impression.

Use the SOFTEN approach

Suppose you are about to make the acquaintance of someone you have not met before. They walk towards you – what do you do? In her book *Charisma: How to Get That Special Magic,* Marcia Grad lists six simple steps to making a positive first impression, which she summarises in the useful mnemonic SOFTEN:

> **S**mile
>
> **O**pen body language
>
> **F**orward lean
>
> **T**ouch – for example, shaking hands
>
> **E**ye contact
>
> **N**od

In real life, of course, these are not steps; some of them happen simultaneously, and almost all of them within a couple of seconds.

Smiling – makes the world smile back

There is nothing quite like a genuine smile to get you off to a good start with someone. It says a lot of positive things about you – that you are happy, confident, approachable, positive and enthusiastic, to name but a few. What if you do not smile when meeting someone? You come across as worried, uncomfortable or even grumpy. That is never going to make a great first impression, is it?

When you smile, others tend to smile back – because emotions are contagious – but you need the right kind of smile. It has to be real. People can spot a fake. How do they know? Because it is easy to recognise a real smile by the upward curl of the lips which reveals your teeth and ends with creases in the crows-feet area around the eyes. This uses the zygomatic muscles, which are not under conscious control – you cannot make your eyes 'twinkle' on demand; it only happens when you see someone or something you like.

Some people give you a forced, closed-mouth, thin-lipped smile – which uses only the risorius muscles – when they want to appear polite or friendly and they do not actually feel it. But we know. When you look at people and you like what you see, that zygomatic smile emerges naturally. Because it is infectious, other people instinctively respond to it.

A natural smile slowly floods across your face and then slowly fades. If you switch it on too fast, or let it drop too soon, it doesn't feel sincere. So when you move from one person to another, give everyone their own individual smile. Nobody wants one that is 'second-hand'.

Some people are great at smiling – they seem to do it naturally. You could be like that too, even if you sometimes feel awkward or shy. It is just a matter of practice.

Exercise

Sit down in front of a mirror and see how much difference it makes to your impact when you smile. Then get in the habit of doing so when you are out and about in the world.

Open body language – opens the door to good relationships

When you fold your arms, cross your legs or are turned away from someone, you give the impression you are not interested or lack confidence. Open body language, especially when meeting someone for the first time, signals that you are open to them emotionally.

Forward lean – shows you are interested in them

When you like someone, you move towards them. When you do not, you hold back. It is a subtle expression of interest or disinterest, and extremely important in terms of the impact you create. As social psychologist Albert Mehrabian explains in his book *Silent Messages,* by leaning forward slightly when you meet someone you signal in a subtle way that you are interested in them. If you lean back, or keep them at arm's length, you will give the impression you are not interested.

Touch – creates a positive lasting impression

In Western European, US and other cultures, one of the first things we do when we meet someone is shake hands. It is often the first and only time business people touch each other, and it is an important way of making a connection. People read a lot into that brief moment, so you need to get it right; yet most of us are never taught how to shake hands. Since we rarely get feedback from others, we do not know if we have a problem – which means we never adjust or improve. Here are our seven secrets for the perfect shake.

1   **From dead fish to crusher**: The most important thing about a handshake is getting the pressure right. Many, many, many people will have an immediately negative impression of you if you present them with a 'dead fish' – a limp, lifeless hand that flops into theirs. Some will think you are weak, some will think you are submissive. Some will even say 'I would never do business with that person', such is their strength of feeling. At the other extreme is the 'crusher' – a grip so fierce you think the blood flow has stopped and you have marks on your fingers from their rings for a few days. Most people ask 'What is he trying to prove?' (and it is usually a 'he', by the way – women rarely exert too much pressure). The ideal handshake is somewhere in between the dead fish and the crusher: firm, but not too firm. Not sure how strong your shake is? Ask a few colleagues or friends to give you some feedback.

    Some men ask if they should reduce their pressure when shaking hands with a woman. Our view is no. It is patronising. What you need is a handshake that is appropriate for both sexes.

2   **Go web to web**: To get a real sense of connection with the other person you need to go 'web to web' – the web between your thumb and first finger has to touch the web between their thumb and first finger. Most of the time this happens easily, but there are handshake styles that hinder this connection. Some people approach the handshake like a gunslinger, coming in from the side, others start from the top and swoop downwards. To avoid this problem, allow your arm to move straight ahead just above waist height.

3   **Shake it up**: Next question – how many times do you shake? One is not enough – it feels abrupt, like you are going through the motions. But for most people (and this does vary across cultures and contexts) three, four or more is too many. So, two shakes of the hand are generally about right.

4 **I'm in charge**: When someone turns their hand so it is over the top of yours they are saying, 'I'm in charge here'. They may not even know they are doing it, but it is obvious to the other person. Some people hold out their hand with the palm facing upwards, which immediately puts them in a submissive position. Should you notice you shake hands in either of these ways, we suggest you switch to a straight hand, because it will improve the impact you make with most people.

Some people use both hands and also touch the hand, elbow or arm. One hand is used in the conventional way and the other is placed on top or part-way up the arm. The further up your arm the second hand is, the more intimate it feels to the other person. The double-hander can send a message of 'trust me'. Beware using this with people you have just met; it only works with people you know well. If you don't know them, they are likely to think 'Why on earth should I trust you? Why are you being so friendly?'

5 **Know when to withdraw**: It is important to know when to let go. Holding the other person's hand too long will make the person feel uncomfortable. Withdraw too soon and they will not feel you are committed. Too long, too little – how do you know? Most of the time it is just a second or two, but the secret of sincerity is holding just a fraction of a second longer than you would normally.

6 **Do not hold them at arm's length**: When people hold their arm straight it effectively keeps you at a safe distance. It says 'Do not enter my personal space'. When you do this, people know – and it creates a barrier to you connecting with them.

7 **Stop sweating and fretting**: Let us be honest – clammy, sweaty hands rarely make a great first impression. It can easily happen when you get nervous. What can you do? Practical solutions will be most effective. Either keep a tissue to hand or wipe your hands on the back of your trousers or skirt before you shake – but try not to let the other person see you doing it!

Hugging and kissing

In some countries and cultures, you kiss or hug the other person on meeting them. The number of kisses varies, as does the style and strength of the hug. Our suggestion is to follow local custom.

 Exercise

Get a friend or colleague to help you by giving you some feedback on your handshake. Make small adjustments until they say it feels right.

Eye contact – opens the window to your soul

Getting eye contact right places you on a fast track to creating a positive first impression. Get it wrong, and you are off to a bad start. That is because when you look into someone's eyes you connect with them emotionally. It is really not that difficult, you simply hold the other person's eye long enough – just a second or so – to feel you have had a 'moment' together. (Bear in mind that direct eye contact is offensive in some cultures, especially between men and women.) In that time you should be able to see the colour of the other person's eyes.

What does it mean when you meet someone who doesn't look you in the eye? They appear uncomfortable, submissive, uncertain or shifty. If they look too long, it gets intense – even intimidating. Somewhere in between is just perfect.

Nod – affirms your positive feelings

When you are in a meeting and you want to show you agree with what is being said you often nod your head – it is an expression of agreement and affirmation. You can harness the power of this subtle gesture when meeting someone for the first time, and indeed at subsequent meetings. Giving a gentle nod as you shake hands – not too many nods, not too low, and not too quickly – will help you make the right impact.

The complete package

> you do not need to own a Porsche or live in a posh part of town to create impact, but you do need to make the best of what you have got and make sure nothing detracts

Everything affects your personal impact. *Everything* – your car, your house, the area you live in, the company you work for, the people you hang around with. So make sure the complete package fits together. Imagine turning up to an important first meeting with a customer in an old banger or inviting a hot date back to your place when it is a complete mess. What kind of first impression would that give? You do not need to own a Porsche or live in a posh part of town to create impact, but you do need to make the best of what you have got and make sure nothing detracts.

Given that you have no more than seven seconds to make a positive impression – and probably much less – there is a lot to consider if you want to be sure of making the right impact. Your facial expression, the clothes you wear, your hairstyle, personal grooming and the way you move and shake hands make a real difference.

First impressions really are lasting impressions. You cannot afford to ignore the finer details because you will never get a second chance.

Make an impact now

● Create a plan to make the first impression you want – at work, at home and socially.

● Harness the halo effect by promoting the image you want before you meet others.

● Minimise the horns effect by being sensitive to what others may dislike.

● Ensure what you wear and how you look achieves the effect you want.

● Use the SOFTEN technique every time you meet someone new.

● Design a complete package that complements the overall first impression you want to make.

Chapter 4

Likeability matters

'Beginning today, treat everyone you meet as if they were going to be dead by midnight. Extend them all the care, kindness and understanding you can muster. Your life will never be the same again.'

Og Mandino, sales guru

Likeability wins elections. Every American president since 1961 has been the candidate considered most likeable by the electorate. During the 2008 US democratic nominee election, likeability was a major talking point. While many voters were impressed by Hillary Clinton's experience and policies, they found her cool, logical and lacking in emotion. Even though they had some doubts about Barack Obama on the experience and policy front, they liked him more – and that is one of the principle reasons he prevailed.

Likeability is at the heart of impact. When Gordon Brown became British prime minister in 2007 he was widely criticised for not being personable enough. Although capable and experienced, he came across as grumpy, negative and lost in the detail. He suffered in comparison to his predecessor, Tony Blair, who was considered by many to be likeable – and, by some, even charismatic.

There are, of course, plenty of successful people who are disliked – sometimes they are even feared. Evidently it is possible to attain your goals without being likeable, but such people are very much in the minority. Research shows that people who are likeable typically earn more and achieve more. You may not aspire to be president or prime minister, or to be a high-flying businessman, but if you want to find that special someone, keep your job in tough times and have lots of friends, you cannot afford to take likeability for granted.

What makes someone likeable?

What makes one person likeable and someone else not? Pause for a moment and think about your family, colleagues, friends. What would you say are the qualities, behaviours and characteristics of likeable people?

What did you come up with? How does your list compare to ours (below), which is the result of a survey we carried out among those attending our courses?

Speak First's survey of likeable qualities

Friendly	Interested in what I say	Honest
Warm	Expresses emotions	Real
Accepting of people	Positive	Cooperative
Caring	Upbeat	Open
Empathises	Easy-going	Generous with their time
Have similar interests	Sense of humour	Articulate
Do not take themselves too seriously	Have good manners	
	Look their best	

It is a broad, varied list, isn't it? And that is because, to a large degree, likeability is in the eye of the beholder. It is not easy to pin it down to a handful of traits. What some of us find likeable has no appeal to others. Even the experts – such as Robert Cialdini, author of the bestselling *Influence,* and Tim Sanders, whose extensive research is summarised in his book *The Likeability Factor* – have differing views. Likeability is a tricky, messy old subject to define, but there are core qualities that most people find likeable. We consider the following eight to be the most important:

- **Attractive**: You make the most of yourself, both physically and emotionally.

- **Friendly**: You smile readily and reach out to others through conversation and a warm, open manner.

- **Interested in others**: You are curious to find out about people: you take time to listen to what they have to say and ask questions to find out more.

- **Empathic**: You can put yourself in someone else's position and consider things from their perspective.

- **Honest**: You are straightforward and demonstrate integrity.

- **Authentic**: You are comfortable with who you are and happy to let people get to know the real you.

- **Positive**: You are optimistic and upbeat without being naïve or unrealistic.

- **Light-hearted**: You see the fun in life and do not take yourself too seriously.

These elements are most effective when they are all evident – the sum of the parts is greater than the whole. When one or two are missing the effect is diluted.

The likeability scale

Likeability operates on a scale:

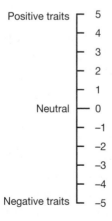

When you meet someone they start at the central zero point. If they are attractive, authentic and display a good sense of humour, and you value these traits, they go up the scale. The more qualities they display that match what is important to you, the higher they go.

The absence of positive qualities does not mean we dislike someone. People have to display a behaviour we consider negative in order to drop down the scale. If there are enough negatives their 'rating' will slip to rock bottom. At other times you may feel neutral – neither liking or disliking them.

Jiang Li enjoys being with people who are kind, considerate and caring. She is neutral about Jerry, who does not display these traits; she dislikes Jade because she experiences her behaviour as selfish.

When we say we dislike someone what we often mean is that we have generalised a cluster of behaviours we are not keen on, such as impatience, interrupting and insensitivity. Some people do not do this as readily as others because they separate the behaviour from the person. Dislike can also arise from one negative behaviour we feel so strongly about that it outweighs everything else. Many people we meet will have a mixture of qualities we like and dislike. We may like the fact that they are helpful, but not like the way they force their opinions on others. Where they are on our scale will depend on the weighting we give to each one quality.

To increase your likeability, and therefore your personal impact, you need to display more of the qualities most people prefer. At the same time you need to minimise those that are commonly disliked.

So what?

Some of you may be saying to yourself 'So what? I don't care what people think about me, that's up to them'. This is all fine and dandy if you are all sweetness and light, because people will like you anyway. If you are not, and people experience your behaviour as negative, you can inadvertently reduce your personal impact.

12 ways to make yourself more likeable

We have sifted the evidence, spoken to lots of people and applied common sense to come up with 12 ways by which you can make yourself more likeable. Put them into practice and you are guaranteed to increase your impact.

1 **Make the most of yourself**: Most of us will never be in the running for Mr Universe or Miss World, so it is grossly unfair that one of the components of likeability is physical attractiveness. You are judged on your appearance: the more attractive you are, everything else being equal, the more people will like you – and this will affect everything from your career prospects to your social opportunities.

   The important thing to understand, though, is that it is *attractiveness* that matters, which is not the same as being handsome or beautiful. That, of course, will give you a head start, but what is crucial is that you make the most of what you have got. We all know people who are not exactly oil paintings, but they are still extremely attractive. So find as many ways as possible to improve on what you have been given. Have your hair styled well, control your weight, look after your skin, tone up your muscles, dress to impress, and – since what people see outside always reflects whatever is going on inside – think of yourself as attractive.

2 **Be friendly**: It may be obvious, but it is still true – people will be more disposed to like you if you are friendly. Smile, and others will often smile back. Be warm and open and others will respond the same way. What if you are shy when meeting new people? Or you do not find it easy to say what is on your mind? Some people do find this a challenge. Realising that a stranger is just a friend you have never met can help – all the people you now count as friends were strangers to you once. And once you do get to know people, being friendly – saying nice things and

helping them – will keep your likeability high and enhance the impact you have on them.

3 **'We're so like each other'**: Most people like people who are like them, so make a point of searching for common ground. Maybe you are from the same region, or have similar interests. Perhaps you both have school-age children, or occupations that match or complement. You might also be alike in temperament – either quiet and thoughtful or loud and flamboyant. Robert Cialdini's research shows that similarities like these are powerful sources of likeability. So cultivate lots of interests, know what is going on in the world and ask plenty of questions of people you meet. That way you will find many things you have in common, which will increase the chances of them liking you.

4 **Make yourself emotionally attractive**: According to Tim Sanders, 'Your likeability factor reflects your personal capacity to consistently produce positive emotional experiences in other people.' While physical attractiveness certainly matters when it comes to being likeable, emotional attractiveness is arguably the most important thing. People usually warm to those who display emotion – as long as they do not do so excessively. One of the most effective ways to get the balance right is to develop your emotional intelligence (EI). Popularised by Daniel Goleman in the 1990s, EI is about emotional self-awareness and self-regulation.

For example, Simon often gets frustrated when his team do not complete tasks correctly, and this shows on his face and through his body language. His team do not like him much because they sense his annoyance when they ask for advice. For Simon to break this vicious circle he has to recognise the part his lack of emotional control is playing in creating this result – and change his behaviour.

5   **'So tell me about yourself'**: When you take an interest in others you come across as more likeable. People feel valued and important when you ask them about themselves and their lives. So be curious to find out what makes them tick. Ask questions without being intrusive. It is one of the simplest ways to improve your personal impact. Listen attentively and actively, and be a 'word detective' – picking up on 'leads' in what they say will guide you in what to ask next.

6   **Lighten up**: We all know people who take themselves too seriously. They agonise over small decisions, act as if the world revolves around them, blow things up out of all proportion, and when things do not go their way they have a sense of humour failure. Sounds familiar? It can be hard for other people to handle if you have a tendency to behave like this. The secret lies in recognising when you are doing it and telling yourself nothing is that important. Do not sweat the small stuff, as they say. Alternatively, pay attention to other people's reactions. Once you focus on their pained looks, you will soon be back on track.

7   **Show you care**: Your child is sitting an exam, a colleague is waiting to hear about a promotion, or a customer is going through a tough time. What do you do? A simple text message or phone call shows you care. It also demonstrates empathy, which is an essential element of likeability. If you want to have impact, it is important to see things from another person's perspective and put yourself in their position.

8   **Be who you are**: You are more likeable when you are authentic. People find it hard to connect with others when they are wearing a mask or putting on an act. When you are comfortable with who you are, you have the confidence to let people get to know the real you. People are more likely to trust people who are real and want to spend time with them.

9 **Be a little ray of sunshine**: Likeable people are more often than not positive and optimistic. Their glass is half full. They have a 'can do' attitude. They are upbeat without being naïve. While there are benefits in working out the downside of projects, if you are constantly pouring cold water on people's ideas they will not want to spend much time with you. Make sure you do not get a reputation as a 'moaning minnie'. It is all too easy to harp on about everything that is wrong. Practise finding positive things to say. You will always be liked if you are a little ray of sunshine.

10 **Turn on the charm**: Charm does not mean cheesy. We mean natural, genuine charm that makes people feel special and important. Charming people place their focus of attention totally on you. Because they are alert to how people react they are quick to respond: they smile readily, build rapport easily and demonstrate empathy. They listen attentively and hold eye contact slightly longer than others do. They give the impression they like you and are willing to help you in any way they can.

11 **Avoid being dislikeable**: It is not enough to do a lot of things right; you also need to avoid doing things that can kill your likeability stone dead. Such 'toxic traits' can be terminal to your hopes of making the right impact.

Here are two of the worst. Stop doing them now!

Do not be rude, uncouth or discourteous: Courtesy, manners and etiquette are crucial. It is all too easy to reduce your likeability by getting simple things wrong that people dislike. Good manners cost nothing. Hold doors open for people, be on time for meetings, stand up when people enter a room, say 'please' or 'thank you', and do not be 'brutally honest' when someone asks your opinion about the latest addition to their wardrobe. You do not need to be rude, even if it is a fashion faux-pas. There is not much courtesy about these days, so it stands out. The taxi driver who gets out of the car to help you with your bags gets the biggest tips and a broad smile from passengers. Etiquette is about doing things properly, such as sending thank-you cards or emails, and holding your knife and fork in the correct way.

Do not hog the conversation: Jane stared into her coffee cup and felt frustration rising while Ali droned on about his latest project. Have you ever been at a party or a networking event and found yourself trapped in a corner talking to someone about politics, religion, death, taxes, or the state of the nation? Do you spend time with people who only talk about their stuff? Do you end up thinking 'What about me?' They ask a quick question and swiftly revert to their favourite topic – them! It is not a good feeling. To create a positive impact you need to balance the 'air-time' between you and others.

12 **People grow on you – or do they?** Have you ever had the experience of liking someone when you first met them and then, as you got to know them better, you found your liking of them diminished – or disappeared completely? Maybe it was the other way round. You didn't much like them at first, but they grew on you. We all know our feelings for people change over time as we learn more about them, but what is crucial – if you want to maintain your impact – is that you are consistent over time.

You need to use all the techniques described here in order to maximise your likeability at the beginning of a relationship – and then sustain your likeability by being consistent in their application.

Make an impact now

- Create a list of your positive qualities. Get someone else who knows you well to add to your list. How do these traits serve you in becoming more likeable? What would you like to change?

- Make time for someone you have neglected lately. Call or text them. Arrange to meet up. What single step can you take to be more likeable more of the time right now?

Chapter 5

Connecting with impact – how to establish a powerful rapport with people

'The friend who understands you, creates you.'

Romain Rolland, musicologist,
writer and pacifist

Rapport is an essential building block for achieving personal success through others. One of the precursors of NLP (Neuro Linguistic Programming), Milton Erickson, once said: 'With rapport, everything is possible. Without it, nothing is possible.' That may sound a little 'black and white', but it is largely true. Rapport is the foundation of influence and impact.

People build rapport naturally all the time. You meet someone for the first time and within a few minutes it is as if you have known them all your life. You just 'click' – you are on the same wavelength, you are in sync. You *connect*. Have you ever had this happen?

Or maybe you have had the opposite experience. You feel you should be getting along with someone but it is all so awkward. You are uncomfortable, and so are they. You have not found a way to connect.

Why the difference? The difference is rapport – the sense you have of being in a relationship of mutual trust, respect and cooperation. You will sometimes get a warm feeling inside and a sense of comfort when you are in this state – but not always. That is because rapport is not necessarily about liking the other person, or even caring about them. Many people get confused on this point. The essence of rapport is believing the other person is like you, and you believing the same about them. You might look the same, dress the same, sit the same or move the same. You could have similar interests, backgrounds, occupations or values.

Most importantly, though, if you want someone to feel connected to you, you need them to feel you accept, understand and appreciate them. You meet them in their view of the world rather than in your own.

You already connect some of the time

In *Social Intelligence*, Daniel Goleman cites the example of a restaurant where everyone wanted to be served by the same waitress. Why? Because she was skilled at building rapport with them. She adapted her behaviour to the various individuals she served, from the 'morose man nursing a drink in the corner' to 'young mum with two hyperactive toddlers'. Not only was she popular, she also earned the biggest tips.

Imagine how much it could be worth to you, personally and professionally, if you were more like that waitress – building rapport quickly and easily with most of the people you meet most of the time.

Well, imagine no more. You already have many of the skills you need. You build great rapport with some people some of the time, but you could almost certainly be more consistent. That is because you are allowing it to happen all by itself, rather than setting out to make it happen.

Taking conscious control of the process will allow you to connect easily and effortlessly with strangers, colleagues, family, managers, friends, customers and suppliers – in fact the whole wide world.

You cannot hit it off with Harry so you turn up your rapport skills to get what you want. While it is possible to use rapport to solve specific personal impact problems, this greatly undervalues what rapport has to offer. It is not enough to just switch it on and off like a tap. It is much more powerful if you think of it as an attitude, a philosophy, and use it all the time with everyone.

There are clearly lots of benefits to be gained from improving your rapport skills. There are also lots of simple things you can do to fine-tune your skills so you connect with impact in any situation.

10 benefits you will get from improved rapport skills

1 People will do more favours for you.

2 You will avoid misunderstandings.

3 Problems will be easier to solve.

4 The deal will just go through.

5 You will get along better with everyone.

6 Others will be more open to suggestions.

7 Negotiations will go more smoothly.

8 Conflicts will be more easily resolved.

9 Influencing others will seem easier.

10 Greater success in everything you do.

Find common ground

One of the ways we build relationships and rapport with others is through everyday conversations. Connecting is easy when you find common ground to talk about. When someone shares your interests, values and world view, you relate beyond just the subject matter. You hit it off at an emotional level too. There is nothing more satisfying than finding someone who shares a joint passion.

Think of the times when you have spent hours with a stranger in a pub talking about football, or on a beach discussing the pros and cons of different water sports, or at a private view discussing art. No matter what the background is of the person, or the context, if you explore areas of mutual interest you will open up new doors.

One way to achieve this is by asking questions about their interests, their loves and hates, and how they approach their life and work. Keep the questions broad initially, allowing the other person to choose how to answer. This might be 'What do you like to do with your time?' You can then frame your next question around their answer. Most people like to talk about themselves and relish the opportunity to talk to someone who seems interested.

Do not make it one-way traffic

Questions alone do not make a conversation. It can feel like an interrogation if you do not contribute your views or share personal information. Generally, the more open you are, the more open others will be. Spice up your contributions by adding interesting details. Tell a story about something unusual that happened last week, or share an opinion on the latest political crisis. Do not talk for too long or they will stop listening. The signs tend to be obvious – fidgeting, looking away or looking at their watch. Revert to asking questions or move on to a different topic. Your conversation will flow more easily when you talk about things you have in common.

Listen up!

Great listeners are a rare species. Although the skills can be learnt, the challenge is putting them into practice. Yet the benefits are huge, so it is well worth your effort. Reflect on a time when you felt really understood. Did you feel truly listened to? You can usually tell because the other person leans forward, nods, looks interested, focuses attention on you and every word. And if they did a good job they clarified and tested their understanding. Perhaps they empathised if strong emotions were involved. Did you open up more as a result? How did this affect your trust in them?

How many times have misunderstandings occurred because someone has not listened properly? It is a recipe for a breakdown in rapport. Mike starts to tell Emma about what has happened over the last week. Emma loves talking and getting involved; she cannot wait to help Mike sort out things out. She is full of suggestions and keeps interrupting him mid-sentence. Barely does he have time to respond when she is itching to get another word in.

Admit it. You would be an unusual person if you have not been an Emma at some point in your life. For most of us it happens more than we would like to acknowledge, even though we know that behaving this way does not help us connect with people.

There are two types or levels of listening: superficial and deep.

- **Superficial listening**: This is where you listen with the focus on *your* agenda. You are so busy making connections to your experience and thinking about what question to ask next that your listening becomes superficial. Although we all do this at times, it can get in the way of building rapport with others.

- **Deep listening**: To connect with others you need to operate at a deeper level. Here your focus is on the other person or people. Be completely present while they are speaking. Nod, smile and maintain eye contact. Listen to the words they use to define a situation – you will pick up all kinds of information about their values and beliefs. Clarify what they mean – it is easy to make assumptions. For you, 'significant' might mean huge, for someone else it means important. Summarise your understanding. When you make it easier for others to get clarity and they trust that you have got their message, they will appreciate what you bring to a relationship. If you also acknowledge their perspective, it will make them feel supported. These are all ways of having an impact on others.

Do not overdo it

Be careful not to go in and start using conversational rapport skills in an obvious way – that can break rapport. People who regularly get pitched by sales people recognise only too well how false it can feel when someone is trying too hard. Go with the ebb and flow of the conversation and keep it natural.

 Case study: Bill Clinton

Bill Clinton is legendary for his ability to connect with people. No matter who you are – a person of global influence or the pizza guy serving him – he totally engages with you. It is as if you are the only person in the room for the time you are talking. That is his 'laser focus' – and it makes people feel special. It is one of the reasons he is often described as being charismatic.

The power of matching and mirroring others

One of the things that happens when you have a rapport with someone is that you become like synchronised swimmers. You start to sit the same way, move the same way, do the same thing at the same time. You both have your legs crossed the same way; you both lean in for a drink at the same time; you both quieten your voice conspiratorially at the same time – and laugh at the same point in the story.

Are you becoming more like the other person? Or are they becoming more like you? It is a bit of both – you are becoming more like each other. This is what happens when you connect, when you get in rapport. You both adapt to each other, adjusting your posture, your movements, your speech, your language – you can even get to the point where you know what the other person is thinking, and say it before they do.

Most of the time this process happens unconsciously, automatically, when people are getting along. Nobody plans it. Nobody tries to be like the other. But you can do it consciously – and when you do, the effects are profound. You make an enormous impact on them without them realising you are doing it.

When you deliberately set out to be like the other person – adopting the same body language, vocal styling and language – part of them notices, and comes to the conclusion that you are connected. The bottom line is this: *you can create rapport by acting as if you are already in rapport.* Most people will not know the difference. You can match any behaviour the person exhibits.

In *Social Intelligence*, Daniel Goleman sums it up thus: 'Social scientists have found again and again that the more two people naturally make coupled moves – simultaneous at a similar tempo, or otherwise co-ordinated – the greater their positive feelings.'

Matching overall energy

The easiest and most obvious place to start is with someone's overall energy. If they are full of beans, so should you be. If they are slow and thoughtful, so should you be. Just get a sense of their level of enthusiasm and passion and reflect it back to them. What you want is for them to look at you and see themselves.

Matching their body language

Body language is the next thing to consider. With a little practice it is easy to learn how to fine-tune your behaviour and build rapport rapidly.

The most straightforward way is to **mirror**, or directly copy, them. The term 'mirror' refers to you becoming a mirror image of them. Posture and orientation of the head or body are the easiest to copy. You can go for gestures, too, but these are harder to follow in an unobtrusive way because more movement is involved. Avoid taking this too far – when you mimic someone's every move and they realise what you are doing, you will lose rapport in an instant.

You will know because they will shift position and look uncomfortable or even annoyed.

A more subtle but equally effective way to build rapport non-verbally is to **match**, rather than mirror. The difference here is that you adopt *similar* posture, gestures and facial expressions to them. This is more subtle because you are not copying exactly what they do almost as soon as they do it. The trick with matching is to wait 10–20 seconds after you notice a movement, then follow suit. Although it is not as straightforward, it is generally easier because you spend less time worrying about getting the behaviour exactly right.

Then there is **crossover matching**, which is extremely effective when you get it right. You match one part of your body with another part of theirs. They gently tap their foot as they speak and you match the rhythm of the movement with a nod of your head. This subtle movement helps to deepen rapport rapidly.

So what specifically can you match?

Focus on body language first. Since most people match body language anyway when unconsciously in rapport, if you do this consciously, people will believe that you must be in rapport.

You can match any of the following:

- **Overall posture**: Match the way people stand or sit – shoulders back, slumped or somewhere in between; the angle of their body in relation to you, or the way they orient either the top or bottom half of their body, and whether they lean towards you or away.

- **Position of feet**: If their feet are close together or quite far apart, do the same. Perhaps they have one foot resting on the heel with their toes in the air. They may move their feet or jiggle one foot up and down.

- **Position of hands**: Clasp your hands together if they do. They may have their hands on their lap or let the weight of their head rest in their chin.

- **Gestures**: People make all kinds of gestures to support the words they say. All of these can be matched. Go for the size or direction of the movement rather than precisely copying it. Match the speed and fluidity (smooth or jerky) of the movements.

- **Facial expressions**: If they smile, you smile. They frown, you follow suit. You can also match subtle movements of the mouth or eyebrows.

Notice the patterns and decide what to match. As for mirroring, the easiest to go for are posture, head or body orientation and facial expressions. To begin with, avoid matching everything or you will be so busy doing this you will not be listening. If you choose to match movements, follow the general rhythm rather than every change, or you will be in danger of mimicking. You can match direction (up, down, right, left), rhythm (fluid, jerky) and shape (circular, slicing, expansive, precise). Size of gestures can sometimes be too obvious if they tend to exaggerate them and you do not. Matching only needs to be slight to reflect the rhythm. Read Chapter 9 for more ideas on what to look out for.

 Exercise

Observe people on television – on chat shows or reality programmes. Observe how they sit, and practise sitting like them. Then follow other postural elements: the tilt of the head, how their feet are, where their hands rest, etc. Watch people you do not know in a public place. Sit with a grandstand view in a restaurant or public area. Copy people you are not talking to – so you are not having to worry about doing two things at once.

You are just developing your skills. Like practising your scales when learning a musical instrument. No risk, no problem. When you feel confident enough with your ability, try matching a friend or colleague for a few minutes. Then graduate to someone you do not know. Experiment. Soon you will refine what is, after all, a natural human skill and barely notice you are doing it.

Every breath they take

Another option, and this may seem rather unusual but it is incredibly powerful, is to match the breathing of the other person. The easy way to do this is to watch out of the corner of your eye the rise and fall of their shoulders or the expansion and contraction of their belly. Is it fast and shallow or slow and deep? Whatever the other person is doing, you do the same. The tricky part is getting the rhythm in the first place. Once you have that, it's relatively easy to maintain.

Most people will not consciously notice you matching their breathing, no matter how observant they are, but their unconscious mind will know, and will respond by deepening the sense of connection.

Diana Beaver, author of several NLP books including *Easy Being*, tells a wonderful story of how she used breathing matching to resolve a conflict that had been rumbling on for some time, and which was in danger of escalating into a full-blown legal action. She and her solicitor had arranged to meet the other person and her solicitor for a 'final' discussion. Diana felt that, on its own, talking would not be sufficient. So what she planned was that she and her solicitor would match the breathing of the other person – which they did immediately upon sitting down. Shortly afterwards the breathing of the other person's solicitor fell in line as well. Once they were all breathing together, the mood changed completely. What had been a protracted disagreement was resolved there and then in just 40 minutes.

Exercise

Matching breathing really does work – and works extremely powerfully. Give it a try when you are next sitting on a train opposite someone. Don't talk to them. Just observe and follow their breathing. But don't be surprised if they talk to you. Unconsciously they will be aware of the non-verbal rapport you have established and may feel drawn to initiating a conversation.

Voice matching

Once you have got the hang of body language, have a go at matching the voice. First, listen to the different qualities. How fast or slow is it, how low is the pitch, what kind of tone does the person have? (Chapter 8 gives you more clues to listen out for.) You can match pace, volume, projection, pitch, emphasis, rhythm and tone. Avoid matching accents, though, as people will almost certainly notice and might take offence.

When one person talks loudly and the other quietly, or one is fast and the other has a measured pace, the difference is particularly obvious. Choose one or two vocal qualities to match – the ones where you are most different and/or the easiest.

Matching over the telephone is more straightforward because all you have to work on is the voice. Someone might answer the telephone abruptly, and then rattle out their name like a machine gun. When you match the pace and energy of their voice they will unconsciously feel you understand them.

> when you match the pace and energy of their voice they will unconsciously feel you understand them

Exercise

It is easy to practise voice matching over the telephone because most of us get so much opportunity to do it. Start by listening carefully to all the nuances in the other person's voice. Begin with focusing on pace, because that is an easy one. You may also notice something that makes this voice slightly different from that of other people. Once you begin to focus on this skill you will probably realise how you often do it naturally when you get on with someone well.

Say what they are saying

Is that all you can match? No – you can listen out for the words the other person uses and reflect them back. Drawing on other people's words or phrases helps them feel you understand how they view the world. Tune into what their favourite words or phrases are, such as 'fabulous', 'get it right', 'quality', 'to be honest'. Whatever these may be, if they are a favourite you will hear them mentioned a lot. Often these words reflect a value or belief that a person has, so if you use them specifically you are acknowledging what is important to them. When someone is under stress they are more likely to feel they can rely on you if you speak their language. This is an important way to create impact.

Backtracking is another great way to create rapport. It is a simple yet powerful technique where you give back to the person the information they have just given you. It lets them know that you understand them. If you match body language and voice and do not backtrack it may not work as well. One way of thinking about this is that it deepens the rapport. It does not mean repeating what the other person says verbatim, but you need to use the same language. If someone says 'We've got a problem here', and you say 'What is the issue?' your response does not represent their internal world. Instead, say 'What is the problem?' or 'Tell me about the problem'.

See them, hear them and feel them

Another way to match someone and create rapport is to listen out for sensory-specific words that people use and reply with the same kind of language. We process information through our senses, and we all have preferences for which sense we rely on most in order to understand what is going on around us. Some of us are more visual, others auditory, and still others have a preference for being kinaesthetic (feeling and touching).

You can tell what sense a person is using at any given time by the words and phrases they use. When your colleague asks 'Do you get the picture?' or 'How do you see it working?', you know they are thinking in pictures. If a customer says 'I like the sound of that', they are using the auditory mode; and if your friend declares 'The pressure is on, hang in there', you know they are thinking kinaesthetically. But do not jump to conclusions based on single sentences; look for patterns to reinforce which one or two senses are their most preferred. The table on the next page lists some typical words so you can recognise the different preferences people have.

Metaphorically speaking

When people use metaphors, build on theirs. For example, in reply to 'I'm drowning in work at present', you ask 'What can I do to help you get your head above water?'. Metaphors are the language of the unconscious mind, so when you match their metaphor you are tapping into their inner world. This is a great way to deepen rapport and have the other person feel you really understand them. Avoid the temptation to add your own metaphor instead. If they say 'I'm drowning in work', and you say 'You will soon get to the top of the hill', it doesn't work.

Finally, match their personal style and thinking patterns. Are they quiet and reflective or expressive and flamboyant? Do they give you all the details when they explain something or just stick to the main points? Establishing these facts will help you think about how you adjust your approach to match theirs. You will find more about this in the next chapter.

Typical words that suggest different preferences

Visual	Auditory	Kinaesthetic
Appear	Audible	Affect
Bird's-eye view	Call	Bear
Catch a glimpse of	Clear as a bell	Boils down to
Clarify	Compose	Carry
Clear-cut	Discuss	Cold/cool
Dark	Earful	Crawl
Enlighten	Harmonise	Emotional foundation
Examine	Hear	Get in touch with
Expose	Hidden message	Grab
Focus	Listen	Grip
Glance	Loud and clear	Handle
Glimpse	Manner of speaking	Hang in there
Graphic	Mention	Hassle
Hindsight	Note	Heated
Idea	Outspoken	Hold
Illustrate	Remark	Hot-headed
In light of/in view of	Report	Irritate
Look/look into	Say	Lay cards on the table
Mind's eye	Shout	Lukewarm
Notice	Silence	Motion
Obvious	Sing	Muddle
Perspective	Sound	Nail down
Picture	Speechless	Pressure
Reveal	Tell the truth	Shallow
See	Tongue-tied	Sharpen
Take a dim view	Tune in	Slipped my mind
Tunnel vision	Well-informed	Solid
Vague	Word for word	Strike
		Touch

I second that emotion

A powerful way to connect is to match others emotionally. There is no point trying to cheer someone up by being bright and breezy if they are down in the dumps. It just will not wash. Instead, slow down your voice, reduce your volume and adopt a similar tone. Match their body language and their energy level. They will know you understand something of what is going on for them, which will open the door to a deeper connection, and allow you to influence them.

Equally, you can irritate someone who is angry if you are calm and collected. They will not feel you appreciate their strength of feeling. You need to work with the emotion first before getting them to a constructive place. Do not smile with reassurance immediately – you can only do that *after* you have paced them. So match their voice – if they are shouting, speak loudly and with high energy first. Acknowledge what they are feeling in the words you use: 'I can tell you are angry/down/frustrated, and I'm concerned about it.'

By matching their emotions first you can help them feel understood, build rapport, and lead them to a more productive place.

There is too much to think about!

You might be feeling somewhat overwhelmed by now and wondering how on earth you can focus on doing all these things at once. Well, relax – you can't. There is too much to think about. You need to build up your skills bit by bit. It is like learning to drive a car: during the first couple of lessons you feel you are never going to master the skill, but by the third lesson you are happily motoring along. So hang on in there. Take it one step at a time.

Leading the way

Once you have established rapport you can move from matching someone to 'leading' them – to getting them to do what you want. You start where they are, and then, by degrees, take them where you want to go.

Suppose someone is sceptical about an idea you are putting to them; you start by acknowledging, accepting and respecting their position, while matching the associated posture, gestures, voice and language. Then you start to shift, maybe suggesting that some of their scepticism is unfounded, and offering a different perspective – your own. If you have gained sufficient rapport, the person should then at least be open to listening to your ideas, and may even be persuaded by them.

> if you have gained sufficient rapport, the person should then at least be open to listening to your ideas

Rapport with groups

It is relatively easy to connect with one person, but how do you build and maintain rapport with groups? That is certainly more of a challenge – and the more people there are, the more problematic it becomes. But the principles are the same. Here are three tips:

- **Look at everyone**: Eye contact is crucial to rapport, so move your gaze around, ensuring no one gets missed – unless the group is so large you could not possibly include them all.

- **Match the person who is in charge**: In terms of energy and style. If you can build rapport with the 'pack leader', the others are more likely to follow you.

- **Reflect the energy of the group**: Are they upbeat, chatty and enthusiastic, or are they sombre, reflective and quiet?

Breaking rapport

There are times when someone continues chatting and you have got other things to do. How do you handle that? The secret is to break rapport by mismatching. Various ways to do this are:

- Change your facial expression to a frown.
- Minimise eye contact, look elsewhere.
- Lean back or turn your body away.
- Look at your watch or a clock.
- Glance away one or more times.

Be subtle, or they may think you are rude. If they do not get the hint, exaggerate one or more of these behaviours.

The power of presence

There are times when rapport seems to vanish into thin air. You were getting along so well, it was all systems go, and then all of a sudden you realise you are no longer connected. How do you get back in rapport? You go back to basics. You match and mirror everything you can, on the basis that something is out of sync. You watch and listen carefully, and make sure you are fully present.

That is the most important thing when it comes to rapport. People know when you have gone AWOL – when the lights are on but there is no one home. Matching and mirroring techniques work fantastically, and you will derive great value from finding common ground but it is ultimately presence that will enable you to build strong and lasting relationships based on rapport and connection.

Make an impact now

- Ask broad and open questions to discover common ground and show an interest in others. Prepare some standard ones right now to use with the next couple of strangers you meet.

- Work on listening to others for their agenda and perspectives rather than focusing on getting your own across. Get feedback on how others feel as a result.

- Match the words, body language and voice of the other person but avoid copying them exactly. Practise on everyone you meet.

- Pace where others are coming from before you lead them in a new direction.

Chapter 6

Influence with impact – how to get others to do what you want

'You don't have to be a "person of influence" to be influential.'

Scott Adams, author, cartoonist and creator of Dilbert

You want that job? You have to persuade someone to give it to you. You want your plans implemented? You need the buy-in of your boss and colleagues. You want someone to go out with you? You have to get them to say 'yes'.

One of the most important ways in which we have impact on others is by influencing them to do what we want. If we cannot do that we will find it hard to achieve as much as we would like in life.

> one of the most important ways in which we have impact on others is by influencing them to do what we want

Think of the great leaders of history. One thing they all had in common, from Genghis Khan to Gandhi, was the ability to take others with them, to get people to follow them. You may not aspire to have impact on a global scale, but you need the same kind of impact on the world in which you move. You can only do so much on your own. You need to motivate others to march to the beat of your drum.

Influencing skills are particularly important where you have no authority, which – let's face it – is pretty much every situation you find yourself in these days. There may have been a time when you could simply tell others what to do, but it is not like that any more. Even when you are the boss, you need influencing skills to get the best from your team. Command and control is no longer an option: you need to be able to motivate people in order to get them to give their best.

Certainly you cannot tell colleagues, friends or neighbours what to do, and clients can easily take their business elsewhere, so you need to tread carefully there. You have to get others on side. You have to win them over. You have to persuade them.

Try laying down the law to your children. Will they do what you tell them? Will they ever! Once again you will need all your communication skills to coax and cajole them into taking their lead from you.

Finally – and this is probably your biggest challenge of all – there are people in authority: your boss, your boss's boss, maybe even your parents. Plus there are others who have power over you, such as the police, the tax office and parking wardens. That is where you will really be put to the test.

The good news is that you have been influencing people every day of your life so far. When you were a child you knew how to get mum and dad to buy you sweets, let you stay up late or borrow the car. Stop and think for a moment about all the strategies you use already. Which ones work? Which ones don't? Where is there room for improvement?

We do not all pass the toughest tests and that is because most of us only use a handful of influencing and persuading methods. We use them over and again in the various situations we encounter – sometimes they work, sometimes they don't. We are not always as effective as we would like to be.

What if you had a wider repertoire of techniques, though? Maybe even a tool chest bulging with brilliant ways of dealing with different people and different scenarios. Well, you can have. In this chapter we will help you expand your options by giving you lots of ideas for influencing others which you can put into practice immediately.

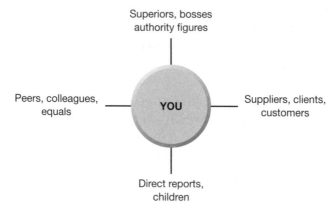

Your need to influence extends in four directions to make an impact – to those above you, those at the same level and those who report to you

The difference between influencing, persuading and manipulation

So far we have talked about influencing and persuading as if they are the same thing, but in fact there are important differences between them.

- **Persuasion** is always something you do intentionally, and will normally be apparent to your 'target'. Typically it involves an explicit presentation of information or ideas, either verbally or in writing. You set out to persuade someone.

- **Influence** is not always deliberate; you can influence someone without knowing you are doing so, or without intending to do so. You can also set out deliberately to influence others, and the fact that you are so doing may be hidden.

Some of the most effective persuasion techniques also have an influencing element. This will often 'hook' the target's unconscious mind without them realising. In this book we will use the words 'influence' and 'persuade' as interchangeable, unless only one applies to that situation.

If the person seeking to influence and persuade is aware of the hidden element but the target is not, there is a covert element to the communication. Is this **manipulation**? The true definition of manipulation is to 'change the form of something', but it is commonly thought of as meaning 'to behave in a devious manner to one's own advantage'. Each person will have their own ethical, moral view on whether – or which – hidden or covert strategies are acceptable. Be careful, though. If someone finds out everything is not all it seems, it may backfire. Most of us aim to make an impact throughout our relationships with others; and this means you need to be in it for the long term, not just a short-term win.

To be effective at influencing and persuading others you need to have highly developed rapport skills – which we covered in detail in the last chapter.

It's all Greek to me

How do you go about influencing with impact? The Greeks understood the dynamics more than 2,500 years ago. In his book *The Art of Rhetoric*, Aristotle detailed three 'appeals' at the heart of being able to influence others, which he called ethos, logos and pathos. Used in combination, they provide a powerful platform for convincing people of your case.

- **Ethos** is your credibility and your trustworthiness. If others do not buy you as a person – if they do not believe in you – they definitely will not buy your ideas. You need to be able to convince others that you have the knowledge, the skills and, most importantly, the character required.

- **Logos**, as the name suggests, is the logical arguments and reasons you put forward. It appeals to the intellect, to the rational mind. Some people find facts and figures highly persuasive – and most of us are swayed by them to some extent. Not having a sound, structured basis for what we are suggesting can hamper our ability to persuade others.

- **Pathos** is all about emotions – the emotions you express when communicating with others and the emotion you elicit in them. *You need to win hearts as well as minds* – and the best way to do this is to be passionate and enthusiastic. You can appeal to people's emotions through the imaginative use of stories, vivid examples, and adding sensory-specific language to bring your persuasive arguments to life.

Would you like to buy one of my ideas?

What you are really doing when you set out to influence and persuade is *selling ideas*. It is not just a matter of giving people information and leaving them to make up their minds. If only life was as simple as that – all you would need to do would be to present the facts to get a 'yes' – but to gain buy-in and get commitment you have to package your suggestions so they are as appealing as possible. Which is why one of the most effective ways of influencing with impact is to draw upon the extensive repertoire of techniques used by sales people.

What do they do? Well, for a start they sell the benefits, not just the features and advantages. What is the difference?

- **Benefits** are about impact. They translate features and advantages into tangible results. They spell out what people gain when they buy something, or the value it provides to them. They fulfil a need or solve a problem. Neil Rackham, author of *SPIN Selling*, says 'The higher the value of the sale the less effective features and advantages are and the more important benefits become.'

- **Features** simply describe the product – they are technical aspects and specifications such as colour, size and speed. Advantages explain what the feature does and how it is better than any other solution.

Suppose someone is selling you a laptop with a 300GB hard drive. That is a feature – and of itself is not particularly interesting other than to computing enthusiasts. The advantage of this feature is that the memory allows a larger volume of music, image and video files to be stored than others like it on the market. The benefit to you is that you can have access to all the music you want.

The speed of the processor is also a feature. The advantage is that it loads really quickly and the benefit is that you do not have to waste time waiting for it to crunch through challenging tasks such as editing high-resolution pictures in Photoshop.

Since people buy primarily on the basis of benefits, you need to focus on what they would gain from your suggestions. If you are trying to persuade colleagues to support a proposal, you need to spell out clearly what the value would be for them. Even if it were something as simple as asking a friend to come with you to a networking event, you still need to frame your request in a way that takes account of what is important to them. If you know they are fed up with their job you could tell them it is a great opportunity to make contact with people who are looking for talented people like them.

Seeing inside other people

One of the secrets to influencing with impact is being able to see inside other people, so you know what makes them tick. As you step into their shoes and experience the world from their perspective, so you come to understand how to put ideas to them in the most effective way.

The better you understand what motivates someone the more successful you will be in persuading them. That means thinking in terms of their wants and their needs. What gets them out of bed in the morning? What drives them during the day? What keeps them up at night?

The carrot or the stick

Most people seek pleasure and avoid pain – that is pretty much universal. They want to feel good and not feel bad. So anything you can do to improve things for them, or prevent things getting worse, is likely to be of interest to them and will influence them. Once you are aware of whether people are more motivated by the carrot or the stick, you can adapt your language so that it is more appealing to them. You can do this by listening carefully to the words they say.

People who are motivated by the carrot like having goals to achieve and are energised by having something to work towards. To influence them, use words and phrases such as: attain, obtain, get, include, achieve, enable you to, benefits, advantages, here is what you would accomplish.

Those who prefer the stick to get them kick-started are motivated by having problems to solve. They are energised by threats and meeting deadlines. If there is an obstacle to overcome, they are happy. To influence them, use words and phrases such as: will not have to, solve, prevent, avoid, fix, get rid of, it is not perfect, let's find out what is wrong.

People are different

People are different – we all know that. It is easy to connect with some people, but with others it is more of a struggle. We don't really get through to them. Why is that?

It is because impact is, to a large degree, in the eye and ear of the beholder. Each of us has personal – and often strong – preferences when it comes to other people. Some like characters who are loud and talk a lot; for others such behaviour makes a negative impact. Some get irritated when people are disorganised or late for an appointment; others find this expectation limiting and think people who like to be precise are a little too uptight. While we often find we have much in common with people we work or socialise with, it is the differences between us that we often find most challenging to deal with when it comes to influencing with impact. The more you know about people the better able you are to tailor what you say and how you say it to match what is important to them.

Learning from the experts – how advertisers influence and persuade

Companies spend billions each year bombarding us with messages designed to persuade us to buy their products and services. Research shows the average person is exposed to more than 16,000 advertisements, promotions and logos every single day. You can discover what tricks are used to get us handing over our cash or reaching for a credit card by watching commercial television and looking at advertisements in print. As you analyse them you will recognise many of the techniques described in this chapter, such as 'selling the benefits' or using the carrot and stick approach. But what may surprise you is how often they work on an emotional level rather than a rational level. Facts and figures are, more often than not, in short supply. The pitch for a new car may tell you nothing about its specification or its performance – all you see is a family of four having fun in the car. The aim of many advertisements is to create associations in the minds of consumers so that certain chocolate bars become a natural choice when you want to take a break, or feel good when you want to have time to yourself. Anyone can harness this power of association by getting people to imagine what it will be like to have the outcome you have in mind.

Robert Cialdini's six weapons of influence

The world's leading expert on persuasion, Robert Cialdini, spent more than 30 years studying the subject of influence in depth. In his seminal book *Influence,* he details six powerful 'weapons' of persuasion, which he has found to be universally effective and widely used. He calls them likeability, reciprocation, social proof, authority, scarcity, and commitment and consistency. Let us take a look at each in turn and consider practical situations where you could put them to use to improve your personal impact.

1   **Likeability:** We have already mentioned likeability; in fact, it is so important we have given it a chapter of its own (Chapter 4). If you want to be more persuasive in any situation, make yourself more likeable.

2   **Reciprocation:** When you do someone a favour, help them in some way or give them something, you create a sense of obligation on their part to repay the favour and do something in return. Reciprocation exerts an extremely powerful pull on the other person, even if you only do something trivial for them. Business examples are the free samples many companies give away, and the free pen charities often send when soliciting for donations. So look out for opportunities to do things for other people, both at work and in your personal life. 'You scratch my back, I'll scratch yours.' It could be as simple as supporting a colleague when they are up against a deadline, or giving them your backing when they have an important proposal they want to push through. When you need their help in the future, you will effectively have money 'in the bank', and so they are more likely to pay back the debt they owe to you.

3   **Social proof:** We are social creatures and we conform to the norm – most of us, at least. Psychologists have shown in countless experiments that we look to other people when deciding how to behave. That is how fashions and hairstyles change and why books, films and television programmes suddenly become popular. Most of us happily jump on any passing bandwagon if we see other people doing so. No man – or woman – is an island. We do not live in isolation. We like to fit in. We have a herd mentality. So we adapt what we do and how we act. You can use this powerful psychological principle by letting those you are trying to influence know that what you are suggesting is the social norm. Statistics convince. If you

want to persuade your company to start doing a podcast, you will be more successful if you can show that a significant percentage of organisations like yours are already doing so.

4 **Authority**: Do you tend to obey authority figures? If so, you are not alone – most people do. We accept the opinions of experts and sometimes follow leaders blindly. We are more likely to take on board medical advice from someone wearing a white coat. We give credence to comments from those with qualifications and credentials. This deference to authority has been demonstrated in the laboratory on numerous occasions, most famously by Stanley Milgram, whose subjects inflicted what they believed to be potentially lethal electric shocks to other subjects – because the experimenter told them to. In any situation where you are seeking to influence others, you can use this 'weapon' in two ways: if you have authority yourself – which might simply be your experience or expertise – you can use that; if not, you could seek out an external authority that supports your case. This is how expert witnesses are often used in court. Even citing authoritative sources can be effective.

5 **Scarcity**: You visit a travel agent to check flights and they tell you there are only four seats left on the one you want. What do you do? You book right there and then. You pass your favourite clothes store and a sign in the window says 'Sale Ends Today'. What do you do? You go straight in because you do not want to risk missing a bargain. Scarcity – whether it be quantity scarcity or time scarcity – motivates people to do things immediately, rather than putting them off. How can you harness this principle? Well, in any situation where you can limit supply or impose a deadline, you increase the chances of influencing others to take action.

6 **Commitment and consistency**: When someone makes a commitment to do something, or takes a stand, either verbally or in writing, they are much more likely to follow through than if they had not. They are disposed to act in a way that is

consistent with what they have said. So if, at work, you want a member of staff to change their behaviour following a performance review, ask them to make a commitment that they will do so. It will then be difficult for them to revert to their previous behaviour. Or, if you have struggled to keep meetings on track, get everyone to agree at the start to some ground rules, which they would then be likely to follow.

 ## Case study: Derren Brown

Derren Brown is a master of influence. His phenomenal ability to get people to do what he wants has made him world famous. How does he do it? It is a mixture of many things, including mentalism and magic, but central to his approach is subliminal priming – a technique in which suggestions are presented to subjects without them realising. If you ask someone to draw something and say to them 'But don't go overboard', a significant proportion will draw a boat. Research by psychologists such as John Bargh (see Malcolm Gladwell's *Blink*) shows how pervasive and powerful this technique is. You can use it in a range of situations to shift thinking in the direction you would like it to go.

Another approach favoured by Derren Brown – but one that is even more covert and manipulative – is 'embedded commands'. Drawn from NLP, which borrowed it from hypnosis, it involves giving certain words in a sentence greater emphasis by saying them louder or changing voice tone. While the other person does not notice consciously, the effect on their unconscious mind is profound. Here is an example of how it might work.

We have talked about a lot of things… *By now* you will understand we are one of the leading experts and *by now* you will be clear about how we can solve this problem. *By now*…

By emphasising the words 'by now' you are subliminally sending a message that says 'buy now'!

Use stories to get below their radar

One of the best ways of influencing with impact is to use stories, analogies and examples. Do it well and you will get your ideas over to people and gain buy-in without them even knowing. Many of history's great communicators made their messages compelling and memorable by bringing them to life in this way. Parables, fables and proverbs stand the test of time because they are engaging ways of packaging universal concepts. The power of this technique is demonstrated by Al Gore in his film about global warming, *An Inconvenient Truth*. In one three-minute section he tells a story about his school days, draws on a quotation from Mark Twain and uses the analogy of a globe covered in varnish to represent the Earth and its atmosphere. Using this oblique approach is far more powerful than presenting the arguments directly. You can achieve the same effect by making your ideas vivid and concrete rather than abstract and dull.

Seven secrets for getting others to do what you want

1   **Reframing**: At its simplest, reframing involves seeing things from a different perspective. It is something that most of us do on occasion – such as seeing the funny side when it rains just after we have hung the washing out to dry. But reframing can be used consciously and deliberately. By asking a question or making a comment that invites someone to see things from a different perspective, the way they feel about it can be changed in a moment.

2   **Use the law of contrasts – ask for more than you want**: This simple technique relies upon you creating a pivot point that swings the deal in your favour. You want to buy a guitar; you show your partner a new one for £800 and a short while later show them the one you really want to buy at £350. It will

seem like a great deal – a saving of £450! – and they are more likely to agree to you spending the money.

3 **Apply the law of inconsequential action – get them to agree to a small thing first**: Get the person you want to influence to make a small commitment or take a first step. If you want someone to join your book club, get them to read one of the books first. Next, invite them to a meeting with no commitment on their part. Step by step you draw them closer to doing what you ultimately want them to do.

4 **Use the 'alternative close'**: Which would you like? The red or the blue? Shall we meet in the morning or the afternoon? The alternative close works by focusing the person on *which* rather than *whether*. You give them two options, both of which are acceptable to you, and thus create an illusion of choice.

5 **Appeal to identity – the labelling technique**: In this technique, describe the other person in a way they feel obliged to live up to. You might say 'You're the kind of person who appreciates the finer things in life…' and then go on to introduce an idea to them, such as buying a case of good-quality wine.

6 **Be punchy, not puny**: What you say has to have conviction. One way to achieve this is through the words you choose to use. Some convey doubt and others certainty. Some people habitually use tentative, 'puny' phrases and others opt for 'punchy' language that is full of conviction – 'try' versus 'can', 'possibly' versus 'definitely' and 'hopefully' versus 'will'.

7 **Make use of the power of 'money' words**: Research shows that certain words such as 'money', 'discover', 'free', 'imagine' and 'sex' influence and excite many people. If you include them in either your spoken or written language you increase the odds of success.

Putting it all into practice

Now it is over to you to put all these great techniques into practice when you are dealing with people in your circle of influence. We have only been able to scratch the surface of what you can learn about influencing. Whole books have been written on this subject – we recommend Goldstein, Martin and Cialdini's book *Yes!*, if you want to take things further.

You can start using these techniques in this chapter straight away. It is the best way to find out what works in different situations. We will provide even more examples of how to apply them in Chapters 10–13.

Make an impact now

- Pick a situation where you want to make an impact by influencing someone and work out two or three techniques to apply.

- Practise at least one technique every day until they all become second nature.

Chapter 7

Body talk – the subtle language of the body

'I speak two languages – body and English.'

Mae West, actress

wo sales people are pitching for a piece of work. Sally is first. She sits up in her chair, makes great eye contact, smiles and punctuates her short presentation with meaningful gestures. She is enthusiastic and passionate about what she has to offer.

Paul is next. He seems to lack energy. He is slouched and slumped. Most of the time he studies his notes, only looking up occasionally. The frown on his face says he is far from happy. His hand appears to be stuck to the table. Underneath, his feet shuffle and fiddle relentlessly.

There is not much to choose between their products or their prices – so the work goes to Sally. She is more switched on. Paul lacks presence and power – much of that is down to what his body is saying and not saying.

Another day, another meeting – another chance to make an impact on colleagues, bosses or clients. Gathered round the table are Theo, Diane, Chris and Pat – and what a difference there is between them. Theo leans forward, obviously interested in what is being discussed, and has lots to contribute. Diane drums her fingers on the table distractedly, checks her watch from time to time and does not say very much. Chris rests his chin in his hands, thinking about what is being said, but his facial expression suggests he is either bored or disagrees.

Pat is the boss – and she is watching all this carefully. In a couple of months she plans to promote one of those present. At the moment she is favouring Theo, and part of the reason is the impact his body language makes, even though she is not aware it is a factor.

What is your body saying?

you are continually sending out 'silent messages' by the way you sit, move, gaze, stand, gesture, shake hands – and a whole lot more

That is the thing about body language – people are constantly registering it and reading it without realising it. You are continually sending out 'silent messages' by the way you sit, move, gaze, stand, gesture, shake hands – and a whole lot more. Others interpret these messages and make judgements about you on the basis of them. Only part of what you communicate is through what you say and how you say it – a significant proportion comes from your gestures, posture and facial expressions. That is why they are so important.

Do you know what your body is saying? Some of the time you probably do, particularly in situations where you become self-conscious, such as interviews and when networking. But most of the time you will almost certainly be oblivious to what messages your body is beaming out – and whether they help or hinder your impact.

Do you have a problem? Maybe – maybe not. Maybe your body is saying exactly what you want it to say, or maybe it is undermining and sabotaging you. But how do you know? Watching yourself in action is one obvious way; just notice how you sit, how you move, etc. – awareness is the first step to making changes if they are necessary. Another option is to ask others for feedback. Get close friends or colleagues to monitor your body language and share their observations with you.

Keep the good, lose the bad

Ask these friends or colleagues to watch out in particular for any mismatch between what you say and what your body reveals. When the two are out of sync, it is always your body language that someone will believe. If, when being introduced to someone, you say 'It is a pleasure to meet you', but you frown and look away, they will know you are only being polite.

Another important thing to watch out for is 'emotional leakage' – small movements that let people know how you are feeling inside, particularly when you are nervous. This can greatly undermine your impact. Most of us have tell-tale signs such as nail-biting, hair-fiddling or repetitive scratching that give the game away. These can be eradicated, and more effective body language put in their place.

That is the secret of success. Getting rid of what does not work and doing more of what does. You do not have to leave it to chance – you can take control of your body language and make a strong, positive impact.

Stand and deliver

Size does matter – at least when it comes to height. Studies show that tall people earn more – $600 a month more for every inch they are above the norm, a fascinating Wall Street survey reveals. What can you do about this? Other than get shoes with raised heels, the best way to deal with it is to stand up straight to make the most of the inches you have. Plant your feet firmly on the floor, shoulder-width apart, and imagine a piece of string connected to the top of your head lifting you up. Pull your shoulders back slightly and allow them to relax.

This is the perfect 'default' posture, whether you are in work or out. You look stable, comfortable, balanced and confident – and communicate a sense of 'standing your ground' in a positive way.

Take care with the 'straddle stance', where your feet are wide apart. Often used by people who want to be dominant, it can come across as arrogant or competitive. Nor should you have your legs too close together. You are just not as grounded. Avoid the 'scissor stance' too, where your feet are crossed over; this suggests mixed feelings on your part about being there.

 Exercise

Adopt your typical posture and look at yourself in a full-length mirror. Be critical. What do you need to improve? Move your feet around, trying different positions. Which is best? Check your shoulders. Are they hunched or are they pulled back? Use the mirror to decide what looks right. Adjust your posture until you are satisfied you have more authority and impact. Then ask others you trust for their view.

Poetry in motion

How you move says a lot about you. High-status people who exude confidence and presence tend to reflect the 'principle of economy' – their actions are slow, deliberate and smooth. It is as if they are moving through water. No effort is wasted. They are purposeful and precise.

Contrast that with people who are always rushing around and gesturing wildly. They sometimes seem frantic, out of control, with a fidgety, nervous energy that expresses itself in constant activity. When they are on the phone they are pacing up and down. When you talk to them you see a foot jiggling under the table. When they are presenting they flail their arms about for no obvious purpose. There is no 'principle of economy' here. All that restless, random movement greatly reduces their impact.

If you are looking for experts on movement, look no further than your friendly neighbourhood muggers. How do they decide who to attack and who to avoid? Various psychologists have interviewed them to find out. The results have been consistent and conclusive: victims were selected almost entirely on how they moved. Those who walked tentatively, seeming to lack urgency or purpose, were the ones consistently targeted. Those who walked purposefully and confidently were left alone.

So if you want to make a positive impression by the way you move, 'economise' your movements. Make them calm, fluid and deliberate.

Sitting pretty

How do you make an impact when you are sitting down? The most important thing is to sit up straight. Do not slump, hunch or slouch: it suggests you are submissive or simply not interested – neither of which is good. As with standing, you want to express dominance by having your head as upright as possible, so avoid leaning forwards or backwards, both of which reduce your height.

If you are sitting at a table, make sure your chair is close to the table edge without it feeling cramped, and rest your hands on the surface. If you have your chair too far back, you will lean in at 45 degrees, which impairs the impact you make. A slight lean forward signals interest and engagement – too much of a lean looks sloppy.

When you lean backwards, by stretching your legs out in front of you, the impression you give is of being 'laid back'. Sometimes this will be exactly what you want to suggest, but in many business situations it will be perceived negatively.

In fact, you need to take great care in general what you do with your legs when sitting down, especially if you are out in the open, or you are at a table where your lower body is visible. All things being equal, it is a good idea to have your feet planted firmly on the ground. This looks confident and gives you a solid, erect posture. Crossing your legs is normally okay, but avoid putting your ankle up on your knee (men are more likely to do this than women) because some people find it aggressive. Restless jiggling of one or both legs will lead others to think you are uptight or nervous.

What do I do with my hands?

Everybody knows that folding your arms across your chest means you are feeling defensive and closed to others. But is it true? Well, sometimes. On other occasions it is because you are feeling cold or your arms have got heavy. Does it matter which it is? Most of the time, no, but when the situation is important – such as an interview or a presentation – and people are more likely to be monitoring your body language, what you do with your hands and your arms can affect the outcome.

These are the times, of course, when you feel most uncomfortable and most self-conscious. Suddenly you become aware of your hands and arms – and you don't know what to do with them. So what should you do? The most important thing is to remain relaxed, to prevent them revealing tension. What you need is a default position, so they know where to go when they are not gesturing (see the next section, below).

When standing, it is best to keep your hands at your side or loosely clasped just below your belly button. Watch reporters on television and you will see that is what they do. It is comfortable and looks confident. Most other options do not work as well.

What not to do

Putting your hands behind your back, for instance, can make it look as if you are hiding something, while keeping them in your pockets appears casual. That may be okay in a social situation, but it can send quite the wrong message in a business environment.

Avoid holding anything in front of your body – such as notes, or even a drink if you are at a networking event – because it acts like a barrier. If you are carrying things, hold them to the side instead.

Placing your hands on your hips with your elbows jutting out is all about dominance – animals make themselves appear bigger to intimidate rivals. Some people experience it as arrogant or aggressive, but if you are the boss, or aspire to be, it can be used to convey your status, non-verbally, to others. Cradling the back of your head with your hands – typically when you are sitting down and leaning back – makes the same kind of impact. Most of the time when seated, though, you will find it best to rest your hands in your lap or on a table, if you are sitting at one.

Turn up the power of your gestures

You do not, of course, want your hands to be motionless – you will end up looking like a statue. Gestures are an essential part of effective communication – without them you will seem to lack passion and animation; with them you can get your message across with power and conviction.

But what kind of gestures make a positive impression? Which are limp and lacking in impact? If you have ever watched politicians on TV you will have a good idea. Having received intense training and feedback, they know what is going to work well, both when they are in front of a live audience and when the images are beamed into people's living rooms.

Add to your repertoire

There are a number of powerful gestures you can add to your repertoire which will help you increase the impact you make.

● A simple way of 'showing you are the boss' in a subtle way is to have your hands in front of you when you speak, with your knuckles facing outwards and your wrists relaxed. This may appear defensive, but it is actually, as Peter Collett points out in his Channel 4 programme *Bodytalk*, 'a disguised way of being dominant'.

- The two-handed stab is also dynamic. Here your hands are in front of you, the width of your torso, and you jab them forward and down.

- The downward chop, with your hand starting in front of the chest and then cutting down past the hip, is another no-nonsense, 'do not mess with me' gesture.

- The leveller starts with both hands in the centre just above your belly button with the palms facing downwards. Imagine you were flattening out a pile of sand – the hands sweep outwards to an angle of approximately 45 degrees. This gesture allows you to take control while sending a message that says 'I am on the level'.

● Then there is a wonderful gesture many politicians use when they want to appear determined. Fingers fold into the palm of the hand and the thumb rests into the crook of the index finger. This gesture has been devised because you do not want to point at people – that suggests blaming and accusing – and you do not want to make a fist because it comes across as aggressive.

Now you may be thinking 'That's just not me, I don't do that, it won't feel natural.' This is an understandable reaction. When we first start doing something new it can feel strange – and it can feel wrong – but you soon get used to it. You put it into practice and before long it does feel natural. What is important is that you expand your repertoire of gestures beyond what you currently do – to enhance the impact you make.

Open up

Open gestures of all kinds are always strong – they show you are confident and comfortable. Simply pushing your arms wide at waist height can be effective when you are welcoming an individual or a group. If you raise your hands slightly higher it is called the 'visionary' – when you are seeking to inspire others.

When delivering these gestures take care not to show your palms too much, as that makes them placating, conciliatory and appeasing – they say 'please' or 'sorry' – and you end up looking potentially weak. This can be used in a positive way when you are seeking to soften bad news or you want to 'pull back' because you have come across too strong.

Avoid the Velcro elbow, where your elbows seem taped to your body and your lower arms make small, constrained movements suggestive of a puppet. Overall, keep your hands open and loose, and your arms and shoulders free of tension.

When used well, gestures emphasise what you are saying and are extremely powerful.

 Exercise

Practise the examples we have given you. The more you do, the more natural they will become. Look out for other role models, to continually expand the options you have available to you.

The eyes have it

In Chapter 3 we showed how important eye contact is in creating impact when you meet someone for the first time, but what about ongoing relationships? Can you forget about it once you know someone? Of course not – if anything it is more critical. Some people might be understanding if you struggle to sustain eye contact during a first meeting, but they will consider it strange if you cannot hold their gaze when you have got to know each other better.

All things being equal, you should aim to maintain eye contact slightly longer than normal to let people know you are really present with them. Take care, though, in business situations that you do not seem like you are flirting. Prolonged eye contact is an important element in signalling sexual interest, so make it plain that this is not your intention.

Suppose you are shy – you find it hard to look at people when you are talking to them. What then? Well, to be honest, this is something you need to work at, even if it makes you feel uncomfortable. Remember the horns effect we discussed in Chapter 3? Lack of eye contact is something that consistently triggers a negative reaction. Others will experience you as weak, submissive, uncertain or even shifty, so you do need to move forward with this if you are to make a positive impact. The secret lies in making several small shifts, each of them almost insignificant on their own, but when added up they produce a profound change.

 Exercise

Sit opposite someone you know really well – a close friend or a member of your family. Without talking, look them directly in the eyes for as long as feels comfortable, then drop your gaze. Pause for a moment, then do it again. This time you should be able to hold the contact for slightly longer. Break off again, pause and do it once more. Practise this technique with several people and you will soon find you are making more comfortable eye contact with everyone – including acquaintances and even strangers. It is simply a matter of breaking your existing pattern of behaviour.

Sometimes when people get nervous they start to blink excessively, or close their eyes while thinking, and both almost always have a negative impact, because it gives an impression of shutting the other person out. Once again, it is a matter of breaking the habit by reprogramming yourself to behave in a different way.

Eye contact can also be aggressive – and too much of it can have a negative impact. You should also be aware of cultural differences: in many parts of Asia it is considered impolite, rude even, to look at someone directly for too long. There are conventions regarding the amount of eye contact Muslim men and women can have – too much can be 'adultery of the eyes'. We also talk about giving someone the 'evil eye', and when people are in conflict they often stare at each other in a way they would never do when getting along. Too much eye contact can be as problematic as too little.

Watch that look on your face

When someone is talking to you, or simply observing you, much of their attention will be focused on your face. So one of the easiest ways of maximising your impact is to make sure your expression is communicating exactly what you want it to communicate.

Some of the time it may not be doing so. What is the expression on your face right now? You probably have no idea. That is true of most people. When you get involved in doing something, such as reading a book or using a computer, you lose awareness of what your face is doing, but if you are around others they will notice you, and in particular your expression. That is because we are drawn to faces – from the moment we are born. It is an instinct that is universal. By the time we are 30 minutes old we would rather look at a face than anything else.

So you might think of your expression as a billboard that everyone will look at – an advertisement that everyone will read – which means it is absolutely essential that you control what you put on it. Although we are capable of choosing – consciously and deliberately – our facial expression, most of the time we do not. We do not say to ourselves, 'Now I am going to look contemptuous', 'Now I am going to smile', 'Now I am going to look afraid'. We pass control to our unconscious mind – the part of us that digests our food automatically and lets us drive a car without thinking – which does what it considers best. But the results are not always ideal. Some people have 'default' expressions that suggest to others they are preoccupied, worried or grumpy, even when that is not the case. Many of us are simply unaware of our expression. It can be all too easy to create a negative impact without realising it.

What expressions should you put on your face? Well, according to verified research you have about 80 muscles in your face capable of creating more than 7,000 discreet expressions – so there are plenty to choose from. But in practice you use a much smaller number, almost certainly fewer than 100, maybe only a couple of dozen. Professor Paul Ekman, the world's leading expert on emotions, has identified six basic emotions – anger, fear, happiness, sadness, disgust and surprise. Not all of these – quite obviously – make the right kind of impact on others. Happiness does – which is why smiling, discussed in Chapter 3, is so important. Other positive emotions, such as curiosity, excitement, wonder and appreciation, lead to effective facial expressions.

There is often a mismatch between how we think we look and the reality of the expression as it appears to others. Unless you are skilled at hiding your feelings – in which case a career as a poker professional beckons – your face will give you away. That is why you need to make sure the words you say match the look on your face. People tend to trust what they see more than what they hear, and if the two are out of sync it is your expression they will believe.

People vary in how expressive they are. Think of Jim Carrey – his mobile, elastic face has earned him a fortune. Think of Gordon Brown, who rarely smiles – his dour demeanour may have limited his popularity as prime minister. Typically, those who show more of their emotions are more popular and make more of an impact.

 Exercise

If you have seen yourself on video recently, you might already have an idea of the expressions you put on your face, and how you come across. If not, see if you can find a way of recording yourself. Maybe you have a video camera yourself, or you could borrow one from a friend. Film yourself talking, listening, doing nothing – then play it back, occasionally stopping it mid-flow. You will soon know how others see you.

A simpler, but less effective, option is to find a mirror. Before you look into it, think of something you feel good about and smile. Now look at yourself. What do you make of that smile? Now think of something neutral and mundane and see what expression you create. What is that like? Play around with different expressions. Close your eyes, think how you want to look, then see how you did.

Change that look on your face

This is all well and good, some of you may be thinking, but can I change my expression? Isn't it automatic? Well, it is and isn't, but the bottom line is that you can change it. It is just like changing your handshake or how you stand – once you find out what is not working and make adjustments you acquire a new habit. This may be as simple as smiling more often, or stopping using an expression that makes you look miserable.

This does not mean putting on an act. If you pretend, you will end up with a contrived expression instead of a natural one. One way to achieve the impact you want is to start from the inside. It is all in your mindset. What you think about shows on your face; if you greet someone thinking how pleased you are to see them, you will end up with a genuine smile.

Get a head start

Have you ever thought about what you communicate by the way you angle your head? Probably not. Yet it is surprisingly important in conveying attitude and status. Here is how it works.

- **Head up**: Having your head balanced evenly on your shoulders, with your eyes looking forward and everything upright, conveys confidence.

- **Head tipped back with chin jutting forward**: Many people experience this head angle as arrogant and superior – as if you are looking down your nose at them. There may be occasions when a detached and haughty demeanour gives you the impact you are after, but most of the time it is best avoided.

- **Head tipped down**: This is a submissive orientation of the head that suggests low self-esteem and lack of confidence to many people – especially when it is accompanied by minimal eye contact. The more the chin is pushed down, the more submissive it looks. A full 'chin tuck', with the chin almost on the chest, is a defensive posture that offers protection against a possible punch to the face. Precisely how people read a downward head tilt depends to a degree on the position of the eyes. If you are looking down, you come across as down in the dumps, dejected or even depressed. Others will also get a sense that you do not want to engage with them. What if you look up while tilting your head down? Princess Diana was famous for this. It seems to say 'Help me, support me', and can appear flirtatious, especially when a woman does it to a man.

- **Head tilted**: If you habitually hold your head tilted to one side you will appear quizzical or uncertain, which generally does not work to your advantage – unless you are.

Each head movement conveys a different message. If you know you tend to use any head angle quite a lot you need to consider how this may reduce your impact. If you are not sure, ask for feedback or actively seek to hold your head high more of the time.

Don't stand so close to me

How close do you like people to get to you? Your answer is almost certainly 'It depends'. It depends on how well you know them. It depends on the situation. It depends on how you feel. It depends…

What if someone gets too close? Is their impact positive or negative? Once again, it depends. If you are squashed together like sardines on a rush-hour train, you will understand, but if there is no good reason – you are just having a chat by the water cooler – that person probably goes down in your estimation.

That is because, like other kinds of animals, you are territorial. You have a number of distinct zones around you that define how close you like different people to get to you. Others are the same. If you go too close – or if you stand too far back – you will make a negative impact on them.

Research by psychologist Edward T. Hall, who invented the word 'proxemics' to describe the phenomenon, shows that almost everyone has a **public zone** that starts about 3.5 metres away. That is the kind of distance you would expect people to be if you were addressing a large audience.

From 1.25 to 3.5 metres is the **social zone**, where interactions between acquaintances take place. If you do not know someone very well and you go closer than 1.25 metres they are likely to react – because they experience you as having 'invaded' their space. Do bear in mind, though, the extent to which these zones are cultural. Europeans in general stand closer than Americans, and Southern Europeans typically stand closer than Northern Europeans.

When you get to know people better, in either a business or social setting, you move closer into the **personal zone**. This is a 'bubble' around the person that extends from 45cm to 1.25 metres. When you are chatting to colleagues or friends you know reasonably well, you stand this kind of distance away from them.

Most people also have an inner bubble, an **intimate zone**, to which only family members, lovers and close friends are admitted. Being physically close to each other is an expression of emotional closeness. There is often more touching. If you are not part of someone's 'inner circle', they will often react strongly if you enter it. You may be admitted briefly, perhaps to whisper something or express concern, but you would normally then be expected to withdraw.

People normally seek to maintain at least half a metre of personal space with strangers, and even with business and social acquaintances. If you do not respect that, you will lose impact. Often you will know if you are being a space invader because they will step back – as you would if someone gets too close to you. You may also notice, as a relationship develops, that people reduce the space between you, which you can take as evidence that you are making a positive impact on them.

When body language goes bad

We all know how distracting and irritating it can be when someone you are talking to fidgets or fiddles with something. So don't do it yourself. There is no quicker way of reducing your personal impact. Here are a few of the most obvious things you should avoid.

- **Touching your face**: Everyone touches their face at times. If you have an itch it is difficult to resist the urge to scratch it. When you do, it often becomes a problem: it makes you look hesitant and unsure.

- **Twisting your hair around a finger**: Women often curl a strand of hair around their fingers absent-mindedly. In a business context doing this damages your impact because it makes you look a bit 'girly'.

- **Fiddling with a cuff or collar**: Men sometimes fiddle with cuffs and collars, adjusting the fabric as if to make it fit properly. This makes you look uncomfortable – whether or not this is really the case. Constant adjustments always give a signal that you are unsure of yourself.

- **Fidgeting with objects**: The pen twirls around your fingers. The elastic band is stretched and then twisted into a tight ball. A mobile phone is shifted from one hand to the other or spun round in circles on the desk. All these movements shift people's attention away from what you are saying. In fact, they barely listen, so engrossed are they in the ballet taking place in front of their eyes.

- **Shuffling around**: When you are standing around, do you constantly shift your weight from one leg to the other, or move backwards and forwards as if you are about to start dancing? Quick, jerky movements, full of restless energy, give the impression you are either uncertain or want to get moving.

- **Finger tapping**: There is probably nothing more distracting than fingers tapping a rhythm on a desk or chair when you are trying to have a conversation with someone. As with all the other habits, it takes your attention away from what the person is saying and can give the impression they are feeling impatient.

Creating your body language blueprint

No matter what your goal, your body language needs to match what you say. It is often the small things that count, so find out what undermines you and work on these. Small habits of a lifetime can be eradicated – often quickly, if you are vigilant. Practise on friends and in front of the mirror.

Make an impact now

- Stand or sit tall with your head upright, your shoulders back and legs uncrossed.

- Use purposeful gestures to emphasise and support what you are saying.

- Respect people's personal space – avoid being a space intruder.

Chapter 8

Develop your vocal impact

'There is no index of character so sure
as the voice.'

Benjamin Disraeli, nineteenth-century
statesman and novelist

Have you ever had the experience of meeting someone for the first time and building a positive impression of them – *and then they opened their mouth*? Maybe their voice was brash, maybe it was quiet, maybe the pitch was too high, maybe they spoke too fast. Whatever the problem, they went from hero to zero in a fraction of a second.

Maybe it was the other way round: you were introduced to someone for whom the word 'bland' had obviously been invented – physically they lacked presence – but when they started speaking you completely changed your view of them. Their voice was full of power.

Or maybe you have chatted with someone over the phone and then met them in person. Have you ever had a surprise that way? Haven't we all! You build a mental picture of someone based on their voice and when you come face to face they are nothing like what you expected. Often it is a disappointment – their voice is fantastic and their appearance simply does not live up to it.

Take David Beckham. He is one of the finest athletes of our time. Handsome, rugged, talented and widely admired, but when he opens his mouth his soft, high-pitched voice creates for some people a disappointing mismatch. What about Barry White? Physically he was not everyone's idea of a love machine, but his deep, rumbling, sexy voice melted the hearts of millions of women around the world and made him a major success.

The power of the voice

a varied, interesting and powerful voice can help you get what you want in many everyday situations

That is the power of the voice. It is one of the most important ways you make impact on others – and is crucial to the impression they have of you. A varied, interesting and powerful voice can help you get what you want in many everyday situations.

At work you may have to say a few words at a leaving 'do', get your point across in a meeting, deliver a sales pitch or motivate your team. In your personal life your voice plays a part in how successful you are at chatting someone up, being an advocate for a cause you are passionate about, or simply letting a loved one know you care.

When you are on the phone, of course, having a strong voice becomes even more important. Whether it is a one-to-one call or a teleconference, they cannot see your facial expression or your body language – the whole of the visual side is missing – and the impression you make is largely down to your voice.

Making your voice work for you

So there is no doubt about it: your voice is one of the most powerful impact tools at your disposal. You can use it to captivate, intrigue, shock, inspire, persuade – and a whole lot more.

Yet most of us take our voice for granted. Unless we have had negative feedback or know we have a problem, we just accept 'that is how we are'. Few of us have ever decided – consciously, deliberately – to speak in a particular way. As tiny tots we learn by copying our parents, siblings and others around us – and because we are never taught, we inevitably pick up bad habits and fail to acquire good ones.

Speaking is a surprisingly complex skill. There is more to it than meets the eye – or, more accurately, the ear. The human voice is one of the most exquisitely versatile instruments in existence, and capable of an extraordinarily wide range of sounds. But how exactly does it work? Well, here is a quick summary.

The air we breathe in through our nose and mouth goes into our throat, down our windpipe and into our lungs. Here the oxygen is absorbed and replaced by carbon dioxide. The air is then expelled by the diaphragm (the large abdominal muscle that sits above the stomach) pushing it back up the windpipe where it reaches the larynx, or voice box. This contains two flaps of tissue, called the vocal cords (also known as the vocal folds), which interrupt the air's progress. When we breathe out without speaking the vocal folds are apart – they are inactive, so nothing is heard – then when we want to say something, our brain sends the appropriate signals and they close. The air rushing between them causes them to vibrate hundreds of times a second, creating a buzzing sound in the larynx/voice box, which is then expressed through the mouth.

Why is there such variety in tones of voice from one person to another? There are several factors at play, including:

- our vocal cords, which are slightly different in each of us
- the shape we make with our mouth when we speak
- how much tension we have in our neck region
- the position of the tongue in the mouth
- how the lips and teeth are used
- our overall posture and stance
- the way in which we breathe.

What's your problem?

You cannot change your vocal cords, but you can change the rest. But do you need to? Maybe your voice is fine as it is. One way to find out is to record it and play it back using a digital recorder or a video camera. Almost certainly you will not like what you hear. That is because your voice does not sound the same as it does in your head. It does not sound like *you*. Typically, it sounds thinner and weaker. That is because we normally hear it resonating through the flesh and bone in our head, rather than passing through the air, which is how others hear it. Many people are shocked when they know what they really sound like.

Ideally you want to record yourself doing something you would normally do, such as give a presentation, contribute to a meeting or chat with friends – something that lasts several minutes. That makes it easier to recognise any problems. You might also like to reflect on any feedback you have been given by others. The table below describes how common voice problems are experienced by those listening.

Common problems	How others might experience your voice
Too fast	Nervous, overwhelming, excited, enthusiastic
Too slow	Lacking energy, dull, slow-witted
Quiet, soft	Shy, unassertive, 'lightweight'
Loud, harsh	Dominant, aggressive, brash
Breathy	Nervous or sexy
Sentences trail off at the end	Uncertain, no conviction
Mumbling	Unsure, unprepared
Strong accent	Difficult to understand
Monotonous	Boring, unimaginative
High-pitched	No authority or gravitas
Cold tone	Aloof, critical, disinterested
Filler words – 'um', 'er', 'so'	Nervous, ill-prepared
Nasal	Lacks gravitas
No pauses	Rushing, anxious

It is quite a list, isn't it? Unless you are very lucky, or you have done some work on your voice, you almost certainly have some of these 'symptoms'. Happily, they can all be 'fixed' relatively easy –

by creating new habits. Many people who sound great did not start out that way – they developed their voice to make the most of it.

So what does a good voice sound like? It is slow enough for you to take in what is being said and not so soporific that it sends you to sleep. You can hear what the person says and the volume is appropriate for the situation. It is clear, not mumbled or rambling. The pitch varies rather than being all on the same note. Emphasis is placed on key words to highlight their importance. There is resonance and rhythm. The tone is just right for the occasion. It is punctuated by pauses for increased impact, and – most of all – it is full of variety.

Getting the speed right

When Barbara speaks it is like a machine gun going off – words fly from her mouth at a frantic rate. When Bob speaks it is as if the words are being dragged out of him. Both have a problem. People sometimes stop listening to Barbara because they find it hard to keep up – and sometimes they find Bob's delivery so painfully slow they completely lose interest in what he is saying.

The speed at which you speak matters. A lot. It is one of the first things people notice about you when you open your mouth – and it is one of the crucial ways by which they form an impression of you.

The pace at which people speak varies: some are slow, some are fast and most are somewhere in-between – saying between 130 and 170 words per minute (wpm). This is the optimum zone for speed. 130wpm is sufficiently slow for people to understand without it dragging, but when you drop below this figure you are in danger of sending people to sleep out of sheer boredom. 170wpm has lots of energy but is not so fast you sound like a runaway train. Those who go faster than this run the risk of leaving their listeners lagging behind.

Exercise

To get some sense of your natural pace, read the following passage (150 words). If you finish it in less than 60 seconds, you are speaking too quickly for some situations. Try it again, this time slowing down and inserting longer pauses, until you fill 60 seconds. This is a good pace for most listeners.

'Variety is one of the best and most effective ways of making your voice interesting and engaging. Aim to do this in as many ways as possible. Speed up to express enthusiasm and excitement (the film star Robin Williams is an extreme example of this in action). Slow down when you want to say something serious (think of Nelson Mandela and the gravitas he creates). Reduce your voice to a whisper, as if you are sharing a secret with a friend, and increase the volume when you want to emphasise an important point. If you simply make this small change you will improve your voice enormously. One of the easiest ways to do it is by letting your passion for the topics you are talking about guide the way you speak. When you care about the subject you naturally adapt your voice to convey the emotion you feel about it.'

Interesting exercise, isn't it? You can experiment further by reading sections from a book or magazine aloud (it does not work in the same way as if you do it in your head) and seeing how far you get in 60 seconds. Then try it faster and slower.

We are not, of course, suggesting you always speak at 150wpm. How dull would that be? The speed at which you speak will obviously depend on the situation. Variety of pace is what is important. If you know you talk quickly, slow down from time to time – especially when you have an important point to get across. If you tend to speak slowly, speed up when you want to add energy and enthusiasm. Once you consciously start to make an effort to add variety in this way you will begin to form a new habit. In either case, make sure you monitor other people's reactions. If you spot the beginnings of a glazed expression, take action by varying your pace.

Would you mind speaking up a bit?

Do people lean forward when you talk, and strain to hear what you say? Or do they lean back, suggesting you are speaking too loud? Either way you have a problem. Research shows that people who are quiet are seen as shy, weak and nervous, while those who are loud are thought to be arrogant, brash and aggressive. In neither case are you making a positive impact.

Imagine your voice has a volume control where 1 is whispering and 10 is shouting. There is a zone in the middle – from 4 to 7 – that is just right. Think of 4 as being quietly confident and assertive, and 7 more strongly so. Both can be effective, but as a rule of thumb, speaking louder will give you more authority, as long as you avoid shouting. Occasionally you might want to drop to 3, or even 2, for dramatic effect, or go up to 8 or 9 for emphasis, but this should only be for a brief while.

Most people who talk quietly already know they do. They have often been asked 'Would you mind speaking up a bit?' Those with loud voices, however, do not always know they are booming. If you are not sure if you are getting it right, ask family, colleagues or friends for some feedback – and then turn your volume control up or down accordingly.

If you are a quiet speaker, going from 3 to 5 may sound in your head as if you are shouting – but it will be just the right volume for others. You may need to re-calibrate your internal settings so they match those of your listeners. You also need to take account of the environment – increasing your volume when lots of people are talking, the air conditioning gets switched on, or when there is heavy traffic outside.

Projection matters

Many people, when they want to make sure they are heard, resort to raising their voice – sometimes even shouting. They do this by forcing more air through their vocal cords, which results in a harsh, rasping tone that is not very attractive. It also tires the voice.

But there is a better way, which is to use projection. This is related to volume, but it is not the same. Great speakers are able to speak normally, and even whisper, yet still be heard by an audience of 100 plus. How do they do that? It is all to do with breathing, and making sure there is enough air in their lungs to allow what they say to fill the room.

As we grow up, many of us develop restricted patterns of breathing – we get into the habit of taking shallow breaths high in the chest. When we expel the air in our lungs it lacks power. We run out of puff before we get to the end of a sentence, and the overall volume is low. But if, instead, we breathe more deeply, using our diaphragm – the way singers do – we fill our lungs more fully.

It is easy to test where you breathe from at present. Put one hand on your chest and one on your belly. Now breathe. Which hand moves more? If it is the one at the top, you probably breathe into your chest. You may also notice your shoulders rising and falling slightly, which they will not do with diaphragmatic breathing.

Shallow chest breathing may not be much of a problem if you tend to be relatively close to other people when you are talking, and you don't use too many long sentences (which requires better breath control), but when you are with a larger group, or there is background noise, you may lack the vocal power needed to cut through.

How do you switch from chest breathing to diaphragmatic breathing? It is simply a matter of practice – of changing what you currently do and creating a brand new habit. The way to do that is to set aside time when you can concentrate on breathing as slowly and as deeply as possible. Find five to ten minutes four times a week to do this and you will quickly notice a shift. To check you are doing it right, place your hand on your abdomen, and watch as it gets pushed out by the in-breath. It is also good to get into the habit of breathing in through your nose and out through your mouth.

 Exercise

As part of your breathing practice, hold your hand out at arm's length, with the palm facing you, and allow the air to project with sufficient power for you to feel it on your hand. Then try this: stand 3 metres away from a wall and, as you speak while breathing out, imagine your voice is a trail floating off towards the wall. Keep practising until you are able to say 20 words without the volume dropping.

One final tip for when you want to project effectively in a real-life situation. Your voice goes where your eyes go, so imagine there is a deaf old woman sitting behind the person farthest from you, and that your voice is a ball you want to throw over to her. Get that right and everyone else will be able to hear okay.

Don't mutter or mumble

It is not enough that people can hear you – they must be able to understand you. If you mutter or mumble and they cannot make out what you are saying, you will soon have them frustrated and annoyed. And that is certainly not going to help your impact.

To articulate words clearly you need to pronounce the consonants properly – particularly the plosive consonants: the Bs, Ds, Gs, Ps and Ts. They are called 'plosive' because you have to stop the flow of air before you release it, which creates a popping sound. The secret lies in using your teeth, lips and tongue more emphatically.

Many people are lazy when they talk, and it all merges into one, or if you are someone who speaks fast you simply will not have time to pronounce the consonants at the beginning and end of words. Pay attention in particular to 'ng', as people often drop the 'g', as in 'lookin', 'havin', etc. It doesn't matter as much how you speak in a social situation, but it can come across as unprofessional at work.

 Exercise

Good diction is important but there is no need to take it too far – you probably do not want to sound like the Queen. Start by saying the following phrases as you would normally, then put your tongue down on the base of your mouth and then say them again, clearly sounding the plosives:

- They were bowling, talking, playing and drinking in the garden.
- Period dramas are great and better than boring television programmes.
- The girl and boy got the big brown dog a bone for dinner.

Change your tune

You are at a wedding; the ceremony was moving, the party afterwards great. Now it is time for the speeches. The best man clears his throat. Two minutes in and you are wondering how to escape as he drones on and on in a monotone.

Many people do not realise they have monotonous voices. Or if they do, they do not know what to do about it. Listeners soon lose interest, and patience, when speakers fail to vary their voice. We all have a pitch we use most of the time – it is called our 'modal pitch' – but when we stay on that note for too long it quickly gets boring. So aim to make your voice more like a piece of music, allowing it to rise and fall in pitch as you speak. This may not sound natural at first, but if you practise (when you are driving on your own or having a shower are great times) you will find it becomes second nature.

Does it matter in terms of impact whether your voice is high in pitch or low? In a word – yes. People with deep voices – both men and women – are rated by others as having more confidence, authority and influence than people with higher pitched voices. Doesn't sound fair, does it? But research has shown the effect time and again.

That is one of the reasons why Margaret Thatcher deliberately deepened her pitch. A shrewd and ambitious politician, she realised that her rather shrill voice did not convey sufficient gravitas, and over the course of 10 years she dropped a whole tone. Her voice became her hallmark. It conveyed her inner strength and authority far better than her words ever could – and it helped her become prime minister.

You too can lower your pitch, should you feel it would benefit you. Once again, it is just a matter of practice. You need to change your 'modal pitch' so that it feels natural to speak at a lower pitch. Do not expect immediate results – this is something that can take a while – but if you do it in small steps, and remain focused, you will get there in time.

Get the tone right

People are very, very, very sensitive to voice tone, which is different from the 'tune' we just discussed. Have you ever had the experience of saying something you thought was innocuous, only for the other person to get upset or angry? That is because they reacted to your tone of voice, rather than the content of your communication.

When you are feeling emotional, people will know immediately. So be careful with your tone. Even something as simple as 'hello' or 'good morning' will tell others how you are feeling. Are you bright and breezy, warm and friendly, or abrupt and disinterested? When there is a mismatch between your tone and what you are saying, people will believe the tone, not the words. Your bad mood, or your anxiety, will leak out in your voice, so think about the impact you want to have when you meet others – and, ideally, change your mental state so the problem disappears.

Voice resonance

Why do some people have a voice that sounds thin and reedy while for others it is deep and rich? It is not about pitch and it is not about tone; it is about resonance – where in the body the voice emanates from. There are three places:

● the facial mask (the mouth, nose and throat cavities)

● the chest, heart region

● the belly, lower abdomen.

Resonance occurs when the source of vibration – the vocal cords – sets up vibration in your teeth, hard palate, nasal bone, cheekbones, sinuses and cranium. Some people are aware of this resonance in different areas of their body, but most of us are not, and as a result we do not make the most of our voices.

When you are excited your pitch often goes up and the resonance comes from the facial mask. Say 'amazing' in an enthusiastic way and feel the vibration. Resonance of this kind can be useful when you want to inspire and energise people, but it can lack depth and gravitas.

When your voice resonates in your chest you sound determined and come across with conviction. Listeners will often experience you as speaking from the heart. Try saying something you feel strongly about. 'I *truly* believe…' Notice where the vibration comes from, so you can use it whenever you want.

Finally, if you speak from the belly, it creates a resonance from the gut pulsing through your body. Sometimes this is too much in a professional context. It needs to be used carefully.

Be emphatic

Sometimes when people are speaking you do not get any sense of what is important – every word is given the same 'weight'. As a result what they are saying sounds flat. Do not fall into that trap: make sure you stress certain words to make your meaning clear. You can do this in different ways: by lengthening or shortening a word or phrase, pausing before it, and/or saying it louder. Generally, the stronger you feel about the point you are making, the more you will want to emphasise it.

 Exercise

Read each of the sentences below aloud and emphasise the word in bold to get a better idea of how this works. The meaning people will take from each sentence depends on the word that is highlighted. Avoid over-emphasis as you can sound too dramatic, too contrived.

- This is a **dangerous** situation – we must take action now
- This is a dangerous situation – **we** must take action now
- This is a dangerous situation – we **must** take action now
- This is a dangerous situation – we must take action **now**
- This is a **dangerous** situation – we **must** take action now

When you next watch television, listen to how good speakers, including reporters and newsreaders, make the most of emphasis to bring their stories to life.

I got rhythm

Music is all about rhythm, and so is good speaking. Some people have voices that flow like liquid toffee, others have a spiky, staccato style. There is no right or wrong – and, once again, variety is the key to vocal impact. Sometimes you will want to keep it smooth and flowing, like a sonorous string quartet, using longer sentences and a lilting delivery. On other occasions you will want to be more choppy. More edgy. With shorter sentences and a punchy delivery. Like this.

Break it up

Remember how James Bond introduces himself? 'The name's Bond ... James Bond.' In an instant he has got your attention – he has made an impact. It is that pause between the first Bond and the James that does it. Silence, even when it is brief, can be a powerful way to draw others in.

silence can be a powerful way to draw others in

When some people talk it is the verbal equivalent of an email or report with no paragraphs. One sentence runs straight into the next ... and the next ... and the next. Irrespective of whether the person is speaking quickly or slowly, we need time to digest what they are saying. Rushing from one point to the next makes that difficult, if not impossible.

Think about it as punctuation. Where you would put a comma, pause for a quarter to half a second. When you finish a sentence, make that half to three-quarters of a second. And go for as much as a full second when you really want to give people time to reflect.

That is the practical side of the pausing, but there is another benefit: you come across as self-confident and self-assured – and you do not feel compelled to rush on to your next point. Listen to successful people on television and on the radio – you will soon notice a pattern. Most of them take their time, and are comfortable with pausing while they think about what they are going to say next.

Inflection matters

Some people end their sentences on an upward inflection, even when it is not a question. This suggests hesitancy, uncertainty or a lack of conviction. Much of the time you will want to end your sentences on the same note. This is a statement inflection. Using a command inflection, where you drop your voice at the end of a sentence, conveys authority, and can be extremely powerful.

Look after your voice

Your voice is no different from your body – it needs looking after. When it is strong and healthy and vibrant you will have more impact. Here are some important things to consider.

- **Rest your voice**: Vocal cords get tired from over-use and excessive strain. This is especially true if you have a job that involves lots of talking, such as sales, customer service or training, or have to battle against background noise, such as in a manufacturing environment. Take a break from speaking periodically to give your voice the opportunity for rest and recuperation. A quiet lunch break with no chatting might be enough to see you through a challenging day, while a weekend might be needed if you have been presenting a lot the week before, with more to come the following week.

- **Steer clear of dairy products**: Milk, cheese, cream and other dairy products stimulate the production of mucus, making your phlegm thicker and your voice less dynamic. Some people are more susceptible to this problem than others. Those that are should minimise their dairy intake when using their voice a lot, and avoid it completely 24 hours before an important occasion – such as a major presentation, pitch or meeting. Bear in mind that milk and cream are widely used in processed foods, and if you are not careful you can end up eating them without realising it.

- **Take care with alcohol and caffeine**: Both are diuretics – they make you pee – and this can cause your vocal cords to dry out slightly. Alcohol can also irritate the mucous membranes that line the throat, altering the quality of your voice.

● **Minimise your exposure to smoking:** We are all familiar with the effect that smoking has on the voice – and this can happen even if you do not indulge yourself. Avoid being around others who are smoking when you need your voice to be firing on all cylinders.

● **Project and survive:** The right way to increase your volume is to use projection rather than pushing more air through your vocal cords and shouting. This quickly exhausts them and gives your voice a raw, hoarse quality.

Making the most of a valuable asset

Your voice is central to the impact you make, so do not leave it to chance. Find out what is good about it right now and create a plan regarding what you need to change. Establish new habits for speaking. Complete the exercises in this chapter. Keep working at it until your improved voice becomes part of who you are. Before you know it you will be making more impact than you ever thought possible.

Make an impact now

● You cannot hear yourself as others do, so get feedback from other people or use an audio/video recording.

● Choose one or two aspects of your voice that you want to improve at a time and follow our suggestions. Keep them at the forefront of your mind until they become second nature.

Chapter 9

Reading other people's behaviours

'On the contrary, Watson, you can see everything. You fail, however, to reason from what you see.'

Sherlock Holmes, fictional detective created by Sir Arthur Conan Doyle

Poker has become increasingly popular in recent years, with many people getting involved. One of the secrets of success is being able to 'read' the other players, to discover whether they have a good or bad hand – and, crucially, whether they are bluffing or not.

This can be a challenging task. Seasoned poker players seek to mask all expression – hence the term 'poker face' – and minimise any 'tells', which could give away how good their cards are. Something as simple as clearing their throat or scratching their neck could give the game away and lead to them losing lots of money.

That is all very interesting, you might be saying to yourself, but how does it relate to personal impact? Well, imagine you are trying to persuade someone to do something – to buy a product, to invest in an idea – to do what you want. You want, in other words, to make an impact on them in a specific way. So you start presenting, you start pitching. How do you know if you are succeeding? How do you know if you are getting closer to your goal of persuading them – or further away?

Most of the time they will not tell you directly what they are thinking or feeling. Sometimes they might even 'bluff' and say the opposite of what is actually the case. So you have to figure it out for yourself – you have to 'read' them to know for sure what is going on.

This is something most of us do naturally without thinking about it too much. Is the other person nodding their head, leaning forward and smiling, or are they looking at their watch, folding their arms and frowning? You are continually searching for evidence that will tell you whether what you are doing is working or not. If you decide it is not, you may try a different tack. How do they respond? You observe them some more. It is a feedback loop in which you are adapting your behaviour to their reaction:

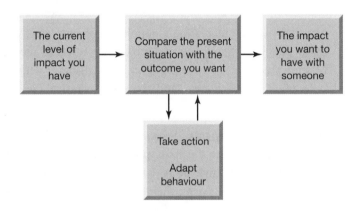

Put them under the magnifying glass

In some ways you are like Sherlock Holmes, Sir Arthur Conan Doyle's famous detective. Holmes was a master of observation, able to pick up subtleties and nuances that eluded his assistant Watson. He did this by using his senses – tuning into the world around him, particularly other people.

 Exercise

Think of someone you met earlier today or yesterday. What do you remember about them? What were they wearing? How did they behave? Be as specific as possible.

How observant would you say you are? Do you notice specific details or do you just get a general feel? Is 'reading' others something you focus on doing, or is it something you do not really think about much? Whatever your current skill level, being observant is something you can develop. All you have to do is be more deliberate and conscious in your observation. Become aware of the things you notice already, and then look at expanding your range.

What kinds of things can you pay attention to? If you have been reading this book in order, certain things will come immediately to mind from the chapters on first impressions, vocal impact, rapport and body language – things such as appearance, posture, gestures, movement, facial expression, voice, and even breathing. Other things that can be added to that list include the language people use and their eye movements.

Cold reading secrets

Some of those who profess to have psychic powers, or who give tarot or crystal ball readings, actually use a range of techniques that are known as 'cold reading'. Part of that skill set is to observe the other person carefully and closely. This is done firstly to collect as much information as possible – age, likely personality style, marital status – and secondly to check the person's reaction to probing statements or questions. The cold reader might say something along the lines of, 'I see an older male figure…' and pause to see if that elicits any response – perhaps a slight nod or flicker of an eyelid. A positive response will encourage continuation: 'There may be some health issues…' If there is no response, the cold reader may switch tack: 'No, wait, now there is a woman…' It is relatively easy to develop these skills – it is simply a matter of practice and concentration. Give it a go and you will soon be wowing your friends, colleagues and family with your mind-reading and clairvoyant abilities.

Developing X-ray vision

To a large degree, though, it is not *what* you observe, it is *how* you observe. It is often said 'the devil's in the detail', and that is certainly true when it comes to reading body language. It is small, fleeting movements that give the game away – and that is what you should be training yourself to notice. The body always tells the truth – even if the person is trying to hide it – and it is evident to anyone who watches closely through what are called micro-movements and micro-expressions. A shifting of posture can show anxiety, even though someone otherwise appears calm. A grimace lasting just a nano-second can tell you exactly what someone is feeling.

Paul Ekman, one of the world's leading experts on emotions, has analysed many public figures, including Bill Clinton at the time of the Monica Lewinsky affair, and participants in the infamous O.J. Simpson case, slowing down video recordings and freeze-framing specific micro-expressions that tell a different tale from that seen by a more casual observer. Ekman asserts that anyone can learn to spot these expressions. It is, he says, an 'accessible skill' that comes from knowing what to look for, and practice.

Have you ever wished you had X-ray vision, like Superman, and could see inside people to know what they are really thinking and feeling? That is what close, careful observation will do for you.

From observation to interpretation

But observation on its own will only take you so far; you need to understand what you see and hear. This is where observation moves to interpretation. You go beyond simply collecting evidence and start the process of drawing conclusions.

By sifting and sorting his observations, Sherlock Holmes was able to solve cases that others had found impenetrable and even impossible. Most detectives come up with a working hypothesis and then look for evidence that supports or contradicts it. Once enough evidence has been gathered, the hypothesis is either considered proven or not proven.

But you need to be careful that you are not simplistic in your approach, thinking that having folded arms always means everyone is resistant, or that avoiding eye contact indicates the person lacks assertiveness. Things are more complex than that.

So, to come back to our scenario earlier, when you are seeking to influence someone, what meaning could you make of some of the behaviours? Looking at a watch could mean the person you are with is bored, has another appointment or simply wants to know how long you both have left – but you do not know for sure. It can be dangerous to 'read' behaviours in isolation. When you have two, three, or even more pieces of evidence – clusters of behaviour that are consistent – you can be more confident of your conclusion.

From interpretation to calibration

The next step, and one of the most important, is from interpretation to calibration – in which you start to look for patterns of behaviour and relate them to underlying thoughts and feelings.

Some days when Jack comes into the office he wears a bright shirt and he is neatly shaven. He has his head up and a smile on his face – and he speaks to everyone before he gets down to work. Other times he is dressed in dark tones and it is obvious his face has not seen a razor. His head hangs down like he is carrying the weight of the world on his shoulders, and he seems preoccupied. He goes into his office with barely a word to anyone, switches on his laptop, and gets stuck in. It does not take long before everyone knows what to expect the moment Jack sets foot in the door, simply on the basis of his appearance, demeanour and expression.

Each person has their own unique patterns of response. There is no 'one size fits all'. Your aim when calibrating is to match what you see and hear with what is happening for them internally. Maybe they always clear their throat before delivering some feedback that might provoke a negative response. Maybe they often speak fast when giving a presentation. Maybe they always...

Calibration is not about guessing, it is about pairing something observable – sensory-based evidence – with their underlying attitude or emotion. This, once again, is something we do naturally, but which we can develop through practice.

 Exercise

Get a friend to help you develop your calibration skills. Face each other and ask them to recall a time when they were happy. Observe their facial expression and any other signs, such as changes in their posture or breathing. Then ask them to think of a time when they were bored. Note their expression, posture, breathing, etc. Finally, ask them to choose one of these two states but not tell you which one it is. Use your calibration skills to assess how they are feeling. Keep practising until you get it right five times in a row.

Watch their eyes

One of the most sophisticated ways of reading other people is to observe how they move their eyes. Isn't that just random? Absolutely not. One of the most fascinating discoveries of NLP is that where we look reflects how we are thinking. Some of us process mainly in pictures, some of us primarily in sounds, and some of us largely in feelings – though we all use all three.

- **When most right-handed people gaze up to their left** they are usually making a picture or movie of something they have seen before – such as a cat they had when they lived at home.

- **When they look up to their right** they are constructing a picture or movie – such as a cat with purple and yellow dots.

- **When they move their eyes horizontally to their left** they are recalling a sound they have heard before – such as the cat purring.

- **When they move their eyes horizontally to their right** they are creating a sound they have not heard before – the cat barking.

- **When they look down to their left** they are listening to their own inner voice – talking to themselves.

- **When they look down to their right** they are feeling something.

For left-handed people this pattern is usually reversed.

How does this help you improve your personal impact by reading others? Easy: since where the person is looking reflects how they are thinking, you can adapt your language accordingly, as we discussed in Chapter 5. If you observe them processing in their visual channel, and start to use visual words and expressions – 'seeing the bigger picture', 'being clear about things' – you will increase the impact you have on them.

Reading others in practice

The following illustration will give you some idea as to how the process works in practice.

Step 1: Observation

You are in your usual Monday morning meeting and Malcolm is once again speaking loudly, staring, pointing and being direct in his statements. Over the last few weeks you have noticed he does this around 75 per cent of the time. Then, each time, he backs off and becomes more conciliatory, with a softer voice tone and less forceful language. The other 25 per cent of the time he sits and doodles, not saying very much.

This is observation because the evidence is largely sensory-based. There is no interpretation of the behaviour at this stage.

Step 2: Interpretation

It is Monday morning again and Malcolm repeats the pattern of previous weeks. You begin to notice that he only gets uptight when the topic is about one of his areas of responsibility or something he feels passionate about.

You are starting to make sense of what is going on, and developing a working hypothesis. It seems like Malcolm only gets aggressive when he feels threatened by others, and is simply defending his 'turf'. When his passion gets roused by one of his 'hobby horses', he plays an active role – but zones out when he does not feel engaged.

Step 3: Calibration

The following week brings more of the same, but now you notice that most of Malcolm's clashes are with Nigella and Connor. His language in relation to both of them is rather dismissive. Occasionally – and briefly – he rolls his eyes skywards when one of them speaks, and you can hear a laugh in his voice when attempting to demolish their arguments.

Careful observation is revealing micro-expressions, and you are beginning to calibrate. There appears to be a style clash between Malcolm and Nigella and Connor. You now realise that Malcolm gets aggressive in situations when he feels vulnerable and not fully in control – and since he fears being outmanoeuvred, he attacks first.

Step 4: Taking action

You want to make more of an impact on Malcolm, and as the weeks have gone by you have learnt that when you involve Malcolm by asking him his opinion on topics outside his area of responsibility he stops doodling and takes an interest.

By adopting a different approach with Malcolm you will obtain valuable feedback. If your hypothesis is correct, you will get an improved response. If not, cycle back round – observe some more and so on until you get a positive outcome.

10 ways to tell if someone is lying

In a recent psychological research study, only 31 out of 31,000 people were consistently able to tell whether others were lying. Most of those participating did no better than chance. How do you know if someone is deceiving you or hiding something from you? Here are some of the tell-tale signs:

1   The person points more towards their own body than outwards.

2   There is either little eye contact or what seems like too much of it.

3   Physical expression is more limited than usual and can be stiff.

4   The person may cover their mouth with their hands.

5   Sometimes there is scratching of the nose or behind the ear.

6   The person is unlikely to touch their chest with an open hand.

7   There is usually a slight delay in answering questions.

8   The body may be facing away rather than directly towards you.

9   Gestures and expressions are often 'out of sync' with the words.

10   The person is not as likely to use the word 'I'.

Eat your heart out, Sherlock

Reading other people is crucial to achieving a positive impact. If you do not read other people's behaviours, you have no idea whether what you are doing is working or not. Once you know what effect you are having, you can take action and change what you do until you find a way to get exactly what you want. With a little practice you will become a regular Sherlock Holmes!

Make an impact now

● Task yourself with noticing as many details as possible about others.

● Create a working hypothesis based on their behaviour.

● Use calibration to uncover patterns in their behaviour.

● Think about what these patterns mean for them in that context – not what they mean to you.

Chapter 10

No more dull presentations – speaking in public with impact

'The brain is a wonderful organ, it starts working the moment you are born and does not stop working until you stand up to speak.'

Anon

Flying, spiders, heights – people have all sorts of phobias. But the biggest of all, affecting as many as 75 per cent of adults, is glossophobia – the fear of public speaking. The word comes from the Greek *glosso*, meaning tongue and *phobos*, meaning fear. It even ranks higher than death.

To quote the comedian Jerry Seinfeld, 'The average person at a funeral would rather be in the casket than doing the eulogy.' Are you part of that 75 per cent who get butterflies in your stomach, jelly knees and a dry mouth? It's certainly not a good feeling. Is it possible to go from enduring a presentation to enjoying it? Absolutely. When you do, it will give you confidence in every area of your life.

Or maybe you are part of the 25 per cent who rub your hands with glee when asked to present. Confidence is an important part of presenting with impact. Even so, there are a lot of other things you can do to improve the results you get, no matter how experienced you are.

Public speaking provides you with bags of opportunity to make a big impact on a lot of people. In a work context you are often judged by your ability to present effectively – especially when you are at senior level – and success will greatly enhance your career prospects.

One word of warning: the better you get at public speaking, the more you will end up doing it. Friends will ask you to be best man, or woman. Your boss will delegate more presentations to you because you will be trusted to deliver. You will even find yourself volunteering your services when in the past you would have said 'no'. Whether this means doing more of them or not, presentations are a terrific way to gain visibility, build your reputation, motivate and influence different groups, entertain people and create an impact.

Everything is a presentation

Many people think of presentations as formal affairs where you stand up and speak in front of a crowd. But in business pretty much every conversation is a presentation. You are presenting when you speak up at a meeting. You are presenting when you discuss a problem with a colleague. You are presenting when you engage a stranger at a networking event.

In fact, you are presenting your ideas pretty much every day, and the impact you make on each occasion is important. At work there are numerous opportunities to strut your stuff, such as a conference, a roadshow, a pitch, a project or team briefing, and a client conference call.

Outside work, presenting may simply mean putting forward your plan for a holiday with friends and getting them to buy into your ideas, a birthday speech, or a committee meeting for your local club. There are lots of situations where you can make a positive impression on others.

 Exercise

What does it mean to present with impact? Think about people you have seen who present with impact. What did they do and say? How many things did you come up with?

Now bring to mind presenters who were dreadful. What did they do that led you to that conclusion? What didn't they do?

The kinds of things you came up with probably include:

What creates impact

- Confidence
- Makes it relevant to the audience
- Powerful voice
- Varies their pace
- Uses pauses well
- Great gestures
- Clear structure
- Delivered with passion
- Opens and closes with impact
- Uses stories and humour to bring it to life
- Uses strong active language
- Speaks without notes and uses PowerPoint effectively

What gets in the way

- Appears nervous
- Waffles and goes off at a tangent
- Flat, monotonous voice
- Speaks too fast or very slowly
- Barely pauses for breath
- Distracting mannerisms
- Hard to follow
- Goes through the motions
- Dull opening and close
- Sticks purely to the facts
- Uses tentative language
- Talks to the screen or reads from notes

Manage your audience's attention span

How often have you sat through a presentation and found your attention wandering after a few minutes? Exactly. It is pretty much every presentation you have ever sat through. You start thinking about all the work piling up, that email you need to answer – and whether you have got time to do some shopping on the way home. Normal conversation is two-way, which keeps you alert, as you are waiting for your turn to speak. But when you are just listening, it is easy to lose focus, particularly if the content or the presenter does not excite you.

The secret of speaking with impact is managing your audience's attention span. If they don't stay awake you will not get your message across – it is as simple as that. So your primary aim is to keep them interested and engaged throughout. How do you do that? Well, you need to grab their attention at the start and sustain it all the way to the end. If they nod off, or say you didn't have enough personal impact, that is because you didn't make your message compelling enough.

Hook them from the word go

Many presentations start dull and get duller. A common opening is along the lines of, 'Hello, my name is Kate, I'm Head of Engineering, and over the next 60 minutes I'm going to bore you to tears with a presentation entitled Flange Coupling Ratio Effects…'. The audience settles back in its seat with a sigh and switches off. This could be the longest hour of their lives so far.

But what if you signal right from the start that you are going to be different? You make them sit up and take notice by telling them a story, giving them a killer statistic or making a statement that is the opposite of what they currently think is true. Now you have their attention – and if you continue in the same vein you will be able to hold it. Here are a few example openings to get you started:

- 'Imagine walking into a light and airy office with plenty of space for storage and meetings. Today I'm going to reveal the long-awaited plans for our new workplace...' Starting with the word 'imagine' puts the audience in the experience.

- '36 per cent of our customers have reported delays in receiving their goods.' A surprising fact or figure that gets to the heart of your purpose is a great way to begin a presentation.

- 'What's the number-one reason why people want to join our club?' Pause and either give the answer or invite the audience to respond. Asking a question – even if you answer it yourself – immediately involves the audience. They associate questions with having to respond, in the same way we do in everyday conversation.

 Exercise

Create an opening for a past or forthcoming presentation that creates an attention-grabbing impact. The more practice you have, the easier it gets. Feel free to steal and adapt the ideas above to get you started.

Hey, what's in it for me?

When you are sitting through a presentation, what is the number-one thing on your mind? What's in it for me? Why should I care? How will this help me? What will it do for me? To keep people interested you need to plan the presentation from their point of view. That means:

- including material that is relevant
- saying how something will be of benefit to them
- giving examples they can relate to

- discussing issues they find of concern
- engaging at a personal level
- using 'you' language.

So if you say upfront something along the lines of, 'Would you like to save four hours a week? Well, today I'm going to tell you how you can achieve that', people will be more likely to listen attentively.

To be able to do that, you need to understand your audience. What is their profile – age, gender, ethnicity, culture? What are they expecting? How much do they know about the subject? How much do they need to know? What are their wants and needs? What are they concerned about? What is their attitude to you and your views? Are decision-makers going to be present?

Sometimes you will know the answers to these questions already. Sometimes you will need to do some research. Much of it is common sense, and you probably do it already. If you are presenting to a customer you have not met before, then look at their company website and ask colleagues to find out what other people know about them. If you have been invited to speak by someone who knows the audience well, ask them lots of questions. The more you know about your audience, the better able you will be to plan the content and delivery so it makes an impact on them.

 Exercise

Take some time now to think about your next presentation. How many people will there be? Who will be in your audience? What do you know about them already? What do you need to find out? What is important to them?

Help them stay on track

One of the easiest ways to lose your audience is to have content that jumps around all over the place. People like a clear, logical structure that is easy to follow, and get frustrated when it is muddled. If people cannot follow what you say easily, they will switch off because it takes too much effort. Spending time coming up with a coherent structure is time extremely well spent. Make sure each point segues smoothly into the next and signpost where you are: 'I've outlined option one and now I'll move on to tell you about option two.'

Start with an overview: tell them at high level what you are going to cover. Then give them the detail. Then summarise. This simple repetition also helps reinforce your message for maximum impact.

There are several ways of organising the middle section of your presentation, including:

- presenting a problem and solution
- listing ideas in order of importance
- talking about the past, present and future.

Engage with the audience

Many presentations lack impact because it is almost as if the speaker did not know the audience was there. They look at the screen or stare into space. It is a monologue, when what is required is *dialogue* – two-way communication. When you think of your presentation as a conversation, something magical happens. You look at people, make eye contact and build rapport. You smile and nod at them – they smile and nod back. They are involved and engaged – and you can see if they are responding to what you are saying. Another effective approach is to ask questions. 'How many of you have had to deal with a difficult customer lately?' Raise your hand as you say it and they are likely to follow suit.

You can also ask a question and wait for a response: 'How many customers do you think complained about our service last year?' People may call out various numbers, then you tell them the correct one. If no one replies, you can answer the question yourself. It still has the same effect of drawing them in.

Don't lose them in the middle

As you move towards the middle part of your presentation you enter the 'danger zone'. You start to run out of steam and they start to switch off. At this point you need to use every weapon at your disposal to maximise your impact. Make sure your voice commands the room – don't allow it to become quiet or monotone or you will send them to sleep. Vary your speed, pitch and rhythm. Use pauses for emphasis. Marshal your body language, gesture effectively and move appropriately. Do whatever you need to do to keep them alert.

Let them feel your passion

Many presentations lack impact because the speaker does not seem interested in what they are saying – it's as if they are just going through the motions. Some even sigh from time to time, giving the impression they are bored with it themselves! People want to know how much you care, before they care how much you know. If you are not bothered, why should they be? When you care, they care.

emotions are contagious – when you feel excited and energised, you increase the chances of your audience feeling the same way

Some people think passion is for when you are not at work. They deliver their presentations in a 'professional', matter-of-fact, emotionless manner. But it doesn't have to be that way – you can find something to get enthusiastic about in even the most mundane of topics. Emotions are contagious –

when you feel excited and energised, you increase the chances of your audience feeling the same way.

Avoid 'death by PowerPoint'

One sure-fire way of reducing your impact is to use PowerPoint badly: have loads of slides, fill them with words and then stand and read them. This will send most people to sleep. It is the legendary 'death by PowerPoint'. But this can be avoided. If you design your slides well, keep them to a minimum and deliver them effectively, you will engage the audience while ensuring you have a prompt to help keep you on track. The secret of success is a technique called read, rotate, repeat. Here are the steps:

1 Stand facing the audience at an angle of 45 degrees.

2 Turn and look at the screen, noting the next point (read).

3 Turn back to face your audience (rotate).

4 State the point (repeat) and bring it to life.

10 top tips for designing slides that have impact

1 Keep them simple, clear and visual.

2 Less is more – do not cram too many words on to your slides.

3 Use bullet points, not long sentences.

4 Follow the 6 × 6 rule – six words per bullet, six bullets per slide.

5 Make sure they are easy to read – the font size should be at least 24 point.

6 Dark text on a light background is ideal.

7 Steer clear of complex patterns or backgrounds.

8 Take care with colours – mixing them can make text hard to read.

9 Avoid sound effects and flying graphics.

10 Use images – pictures and graphs add clarity and interest.

Some people use notes as well as slides, but this is dangerous – it is a double distraction and can lead to you giving the audience little or no eye contact. Use one or the other, not both. If you do use notes, make sure that is what they are: key points, single words or fragments, which you can quickly glance at. Avoid writing out a script because it is harder to read and you are likely to spend most of your time looking down rather than at your audience. After a little practice you will be amazed at how easy and liberating you find delivering a presentation without any notes at all.

Bring your ideas to life

You can do all of these things – get the structure right, speak with passion, maintain eye contact – and still it's dull. To present with impact you need to paint pictures in people's minds. Tell them a story, use examples and case studies, share an anecdote.

Compare these examples:

- 'Our software is reliable and will save your people time.'

- 'One of our clients, Fred Baxendale from CH Car Hire, installed the new software system three months ago. He said it was one of the best decisions he ever made. It has reduced his workforce's down time by 10 per cent.'

Which one holds your attention and gets the message across with impact? It is obvious: the best stories and illustrations come from personal experience. Keep them brief and to the point. If they ramble on too long, people lose interest.

Metaphors are another great way of adding a little spice to your presentation: 'The new meeting room is an oasis of peace when you need to get some work done.' The richer your language, the more impact you make.

Exercise

Create a case study or story you can incorporate into your next presentation. Practise telling the story a few times to family or friends until it flows easily.

Mesmerise them with the magic of your words

Martin Luther King is best remembered for his 'I have a dream' speech about racial equality, delivered in Washington in 1963. Like many great speakers, he used rhetorical techniques developed by the Greeks to mesmerise and influence. There are lots of techniques. Here are just a few to get you started.

- **Repetition**: Martin Luther King repeated the 'I have a dream' refrain several times.
- **Antithesis**: This is about contrast – this, not that. 'We're not the biggest, but we are the best. We're not looking to be all things to all men, we want to be the leaders in our specialist sector.'
- **Tripling**: The rule of three, otherwise known as tripling, is a useful, well-known and effective technique. 'We need to consider time, cost and quality.' 'This book will give you impact, confidence and success.'
- **Alliteration**: Another colourful technique, where the first letter of each word is the same – 'The dark days have disappeared' is one example.

Any questions?

Success in the question and answer session is crucial. Why? Because it is one of the parts people most remember. Deliver a great presentation then struggle with the Q&A and you will leave a poor lasting impression. Deliver an average presentation and answer the questions brilliantly and you will probably get congratulated. So anticipate what you are likely to be asked and know how you are going to respond. Some people look forward to answering questions because it is more like a real

if you have prepared well, you have nothing to fear

conversation and they get a response. Others dread it because they are worried about something difficult coming out of left-field that they cannot answer. If you have prepared well, you have nothing to fear. If you get a tough one and you are not sure of the answer, there is no shame in saying you will find out and get back to them.

Pulling the threads together

The most important thing is not to end with questions. To close your presentation with impact – and rescue it if the last question was problematic – you need to briefly recap your key messages, add a 'call to action' and leave them with a clear final thought. The 'call to action' can be just to ask them to think about what you have said, or a request for them to actually do something afterwards. You can use the list of ideas we covered on how to open your presentation as a source of inspiration for your close.

Practice – and rehearsal – make perfect

Preparation is essential to success in presenting – and so is practice. The more public speaking you do, the better you will get. You will enhance your reputation, appear credible, and get buy-in to your ideas. A vital part of preparation is rehearsal. Many people don't bother – and it shows. They often run over time and do not express things well because they are searching for the right words. It is better if you practise out loud. If you do not have much time – who does these days? – run through it in your mind a few times to make sure you have got the flow right.

Don't forget the logistics

After all your hard work make sure you don't fall at the final hurdle – the logistics. Check you know how the projector and other equipment works. Get to the room nice and early if you can, so you have a chance to set things up how you want them. Take a back-up copy of your slides with you if you are presenting somewhere you have not been before.

Stand out from the crowd

Since most presentations are mediocre and lack impact it isn't hard to be in the top 20 per cent of presenters. We have given you lots of tried-and-tested techniques to use. If you only try half of them, your presentations will improve enormously. If you are determined and want to stand out from the crowd, there is no reason why you cannot win a gold and present with real impact.

Make an impact now

- Reflect on the last presentation you delivered and think of two or three things you could do to create more impact.

- Get someone you trust to give you feedback when you next present so you know what you need to work on.

- Add an attention-grabbing opening and a story or metaphor to your next presentation.

Chapter 11

Speak up, speak out – making an impact in meetings

'Look at every meeting as an opportunity to fulfil your dream.'

Anon

M eetings, meetings, meetings – sometimes it seems like all you do is attend meetings. Well, that is probably true for some of you. Others may be lucky and avoid the maddening tedium that many of us experience when we attend them. The business guru Kenneth Blanchard famously said, 'Some people refer to meetings as a place where you take minutes and waste hours.' While this may be an exaggeration, many people do feel they attend too many meetings and think they spend too much valuable time in them. Nevertheless, communication in most companies revolves around meetings so you need to be able to participate, contribute and make an impact. They are a great place to raise your profile and get buy-in to your ideas. How you present yourself in them can make a big difference to your career prospects at work. Get it wrong and you are in danger of reducing your impact and limiting your potential for success.

Handling nerves, feeling confident

Many people feel nervous about contributing to discussions at meetings. This may be because they are afraid of saying the wrong thing, sounding as if they do not know what they are talking about, or upsetting others by causing conflict. Here are some simple, practical ways of feeling more confident in speaking out.

- **Realise people are on your side**: Although there is sometimes disagreement and even conflict, this is rarely personal. Rather it is people arguing or fighting for causes they feel strongly about. Once you appreciate that they are not having a go at you, only challenging what you are saying, you can more confidently make suggestions and express opinions.

- **Don't feel you have to say it perfectly**: Do not expect to say things clearly every time. What you have to say may come out a bit muddled sometimes, and that is true for everyone. If you miss something out, you can always add it later. If you get it slightly wrong, you can still clarify your point.

- **Manage your state**: If you have a tendency to get anxious during a meeting – perhaps even 'panic' when the spotlight falls on you – there are ways you can manage your state and keep your emotions under control. You can remain cool, calm and collected by breathing deeply, expecting a positive outcome, and remembering you have as much right to offer your opinions as anyone else.

- **Chat to others before it starts**: Getting there ahead of time so you can talk to other people beforehand will help you feel comfortable with them. This is especially true if you are meeting them for the first time. Once you build rapport you can talk to people more easily.

- **Prepare, prepare, prepare**: The more you prepare for a meeting, knowing what you want from it and where you stand on key items of the agenda, the more confident you will be in putting forward your views and ideas. And, in the ebb and flow of the meeting, you'll find it easier to chip in with comments.

This is especially useful if you care about getting things right and therefore worry about making mistakes. Being prepared means that you can put your ideas across in the best possible way and get the agreement of the people that you want to influence in the room.

Preparation is also important if you are an extrovert, because extroverts have the tendency to think on their feet and blurt out ideas which haven't been fully formed. Spend a bit of time in preparation and you can make sure you and your ideas are taken more seriously.

So take some time to consider what you want to say, perhaps making a few brief notes you can refer to during the meeting, should your mind suddenly go blank. If there's an agenda make a start on this as soon as you receive it. If not, the purpose of the meeting will give you a clue.

With regular events, such as team meetings, think about issues that will help you or others with their work.

- **Create a plan of attack**: Make sure you are clear about the purpose of the meeting. Define a realistic, specific and measurable personal objective for what you will have achieved by the end of the meeting (for example, 'I will gain agreement to implement the new form I have created to streamline the administrative process'). Decide on the information or materials you will need to put across to achieve your objective – and plan to convey it clearly and concisely. Be ready to back up your ideas with research or other evidence where possible. Try and put yourself in your colleagues' shoes – if you were them, how would you react to your recommendations? What additional information or data will they need to make a decision? You may choose to circulate background reading beforehand, if you think this will mean people have more time to consider your idea thoroughly. Be aware that this also allows them time to come up with counter-arguments. Try to anticipate any problems and how you might deal with them if they arise. If you know you will encounter resistance, spend some time lobbying for support. Create a fan club for your idea.

Finally, think about the impression you want to convey and how you plan to build rapport.

Exercise

Make some notes now about the next meeting you are due to attend. Gather the information you need and anticipate any potential problems.

Where you sit matters

Where you sit at a meeting can make a big difference to the impact you make. In one-to-one meetings, sitting opposite someone can be interpreted as challenging, side-by-side suggests you are collaborating, and sitting at right-angles to the other person comes across as supportive.

For larger groups where there is a round table it does not matter where you sit. With oblong or square tables it is useful to position yourself where you can catch the Chair's eye fairly easily. This increases the odds of you getting an opportunity to speak. The Chair sometimes sits at the head of the table, which is one way they assert their authority. At formal meetings those farthest away are sometimes the least senior or influential. When the Chair sits on one side of the table – often in the middle – those opposite are in a naturally confronting position, particularly the person directly opposite. In large meetings, the closer you are towards the centre of the table, the easier it will be to contribute.

Communicating with impact in meetings

One of the first things people notice about you in meetings is your body language. As we discussed in Chapter 7, aim to sit upright with your shoulders back, especially when you are speaking. Leaning forward slightly makes you look alert and engaged. When you relax, make sure you do not slump – it can give the impression you are not bothered. If you want to convey interest in what someone is saying, you need to keep your body still, lean forward slightly and focus on what they are doing and saying.

To speak or not to speak – *when* is the question?

The longer you wait before opening your mouth at a meeting, the more pressure you will feel to say something earth-shatteringly valuable. Delaying it can make you even more anxious. Aim to say something in the first few minutes. This can require grit and determination for some people – especially when they are surrounded by lots of strong characters. Using the previous speaker's name can be a powerful way of gaining their attention. State firmly that you have something to add and do not give up until you have got your message across. If you still cannot get a word in edgeway, make eye contact with the Chair (if there is one) and they should come to your aid.

If you cannot think of anything appropriate to say, agree with the previous speaker or add to a point they have made.

Avoid interrupting others and do not let them interrupt you. Make a note of any queries you have and raise your points when they have finished speaking. If they butt in mid-flow, look them in the eye, use their name and tell them you have not finished. Use language such as 'I am interested in what you have to say, but I'll complete my point first', or 'I would like you to make a note of that question because I want to ask me again later'. The only person who has this right to interrupt is the Chair.

Communicate your point with confidence

Acting as if you are confident, or using other techniques from Chapter 1, will help you deliver a convincing argument. Make sure your voice is firm and audible. Keep your input short, to the point and relevant. Make no more than two points per contribution, to allow time for others to speak. Do not put forward an opinion on every issue – speak when you have something relevant to say. Equally, do not save everything up for the end of the meeting – come in when there is a natural break if you can.

Let them know what you think

This may sound obvious, but you will improve your chances of achieving your outcome if you say clearly and precisely what you want. Be proactive and let them know about your ideas and recommendations. People are not mind-readers. If you do not let others know what you want, no one else will. Do not assume they will know what matters to you or your department. Use positive language such as: 'I would like to…', 'I want us to…', 'I know', or 'I believe'.

If you disagree with what someone says, do not hold back. It serves no one. When you have a different opinion, draw attention to it and offer an alternative solution with the reasons why. Equally, let people know when you agree; this helps move things in the direction you want them to go. It is the weight of opinion that carries recommendations through. If you realise you are wrong once you have listened to all the arguments, be prepared to concede.

Roger Mosvick and Robert Nelson, authors of *We've Got to Start Meeting Like This!*, created a simple but effective method to make sure you get your ideas across effectively, called the impact formula.

The impact formula

1 **State your idea**: 'I think we need to consider option one more fully before we make up our minds to go for option two.'

2 **Relate it to what has just been said**: 'While option two has many merits, it doesn't completely satisfy our need to reduce the number of customer complaints about responsiveness.'

3 **Support your idea with evidence**: 'The quality
measurement survey suggests there are a number of issues we
need to consider...' Go on to back this up with specific data to
support your case. Be sure to use the influencing techniques in
Chapter 6 to help you get buy-in. Social proof works well at this
stage – people will do things that they see other people doing.

4 **Integrate your comment into the discussion**: 'The data
suggests that while both options have much to commend them,
there are more risks attached to option two. Do you agree with
this conclusion?'

 Exercise

Prepare the case for a pet project where you can use the impact formula.
Come up with a succinct and clear explanation of your idea. Gather evidence
to support your thinking.

Practise describing your case (step 1) and then add the evidence (step 3). Ask a
friend to give you feedback on the way you express your case. Encourage them
to ask questions if they do not understated. You will not be able to rehearse the
whole thing but it helps a lot to be clear on how you want to express your ideas.

Nothing to say?

You may, like many other people, have times during meetings
when you have nothing much to say. This does not mean you
cannot make an impact. When you do not have a strong view on
the topic, or it is not relevant to you, support others by agreeing
with them – 'Great suggestion, Joe, I'd support that.' If you decide
to challenge them, you need to have well thought through
arguments to back up your position. Alternatively, focus your
attention on helping the Chair manage the process. Seek to do
something positive to support the group.

It is worth being aware that if you believe it is better to keep quiet than disagree, you are being non-assertive. If you say 'I do not mind' you make it harder for the other person to make a fair decision because they do not know if you really have a preference. Some people confuse non-assertion with being polite and helpful. You need to be confident and assertive in meetings. Do not let people talk over you.

Many meetings, many opportunities

Meetings come in different shapes and forms. They can be formal or informal. They involve your immediate team, bosses, colleagues, customers, suppliers, partners, friends, associates and shareholders. They can be one-on-one or with a large group of people. The most important factor, though, is the impression you make on those who attend.

There are various types of meetings:

- performance
- sales
- account management
- team meetings or briefings
- departmental
- board
- annual general
- public.

Work-related meetings can obviously be internal or external. We often place more emphasis on external meetings – where there is lots at stake, such as a client pitch – even though internal meetings are one of the best ways to get seen by a wider range of people. To make an impact you need to raise your visibility. Whatever the situation, a meeting provides you with a golden opportunity to shine.

In some meetings the contribution you can make will be limited, such as a cascade meeting to a whole department or a team briefing. This type of gathering is usually designed to pass on information with no or limited discussion. The impact you can make depends upon your role. If you are running the meeting much depends on how you cascade the information. (See Chapter 10 for advice on how to make an impact when presenting.) Even so, you can either slump in your chair with your head in your hands and appear bored by the proceedings, or be alert, sit upright and look as if you are paying attention. We realise this can be a real challenge if the person speaking drones on and on and on about something that does not affect you, but if you make the effort people will associate you with being the sort of person who takes an interest in things and gets involved. Ask an intelligent question if there is a Q&A session at the end, even if it is simply to clarify a point you were not sure about. Do not hog the air time by asking too many questions in a row, though – other people are often irritated by this type of behaviour. One or two questions and a positive comment about what you have heard are about right.

More typically, meetings have an agenda, although some do not and tend to be more free-flowing and informal. In either case, all attendees are expected to contribute. The purpose of meetings vary, such as dealing with information, feeding back on a project, resolving problems, making decisions and coming up with creative ideas or solutions. All provide great opportunities for you to make a contribution and an impact.

In fact, you are always making an impact – even when you are sitting there saying nothing. If you are talking non-stop you are creating a different kind of impression. At either extreme the result is potentially negative. It is not so much about the quantity of your contribution, it is the quality that matters – it is better to say one useful thing than ten that are not.

Make an impact in the Chair's role

Those who chair meetings get an excellent opportunity to demonstrate their leadership and communication skills. When they do it well, they will undoubtedly create a positive impact. Think of people you know who have chaired meetings you have attended. Which ones stand out in your mind, and for what reason? Compare your experience with these two scenarios.

Roy takes charge from the start. His humour and light, yet firm, touch keep things moving. He makes sure everyone has a chance to speak and even manages to keep chatty Cathy in check. He makes sure each agreement is recorded and actions are minuted. Better still, we get through the agenda in record time.

Paula always arrives in a rush and seems totally disorganised. In some ways she might as well not be there because she has little influence over the others. Jatinder doesn't get a look in. Sometimes she only remembers to look at the actions from the previous meeting halfway through. After a while Kate rescues us all by surreptitiously taking over.

Do either of these sound familiar? The average meeting is probably somewhere in between the two. When you run a meeting efficiently you will make an impact. The value you add is not so much about making a contribution – your role is to manage the process. This means making sure people do not talk too much and the quieter ones are included. If you have strong feelings about something on the agenda it is better to ask someone else to chair that item. It is also your responsibility to make sure action points are noted.

One thing is clear: if you do a good job you will win the respect and admiration of others. They will want to attend your meetings and you will create a reputation as someone with impact.

Before the meeting

When chairing a meeting, be sure to get the agenda out well ahead of time. This allows people to prepare effectively for the meeting. Follow the hints and tips below to make sure you get off to a good start:

- Avoid scheduling a meeting straight after lunch when energy can dip.
- Only invite people who need to be there – people complain when a meeting is not relevant to them.
- Include details of the time, place and purpose.
- Keep the agenda as short as possible.
- Place the most important issues at the start when energy is at its highest.
- Allow enough time to cover the items without rushing through them too quickly.
- Be generous on the amount of time you allow – nobody will mind if the meeting finishes early.

The art of inclusion

Everyone who attends a meeting has the potential to contribute something valuable, given the chance. Really good Chairs master the art of making sure everyone is heard. This does not mean everyone needs to say something about every agenda item. If someone is silent, think about possible reasons for them keeping quiet before inviting them to speak. Sometimes shy or more junior people are reluctant to join in for fear of looking foolish or getting something wrong. Should you suspect this, tell them in advance you will be asking their opinion on a specific topic. By giving them time to prepare you are more likely to get a response. Even where this is not possible, you can ask them to share their experience on subjects where they have relevant knowledge of the subject. 'Liam, I know you have had a lot of experience with office reorganisations and have done some research into how it could affect us. Can you tell us about it?' Use open questions: 'Sam, how will that affect your team?', 'James, what do you think about that?' Shy people may find it easier to talk about facts than opinions.

Order, order, order

Most people behave well in meetings, but an effective Chair should be prepared to take action on the few occasions where things get out of hand. People can be disruptive in a number of ways. One common problem is when someone does not follow through on a task they said they would complete. If this happens, remind them they will be expected to complete it by the next meeting. If this persists, ask them what prevented them from doing it. Sometimes there may be a good reason. If not, it is likely that they have not bought into the idea fully so you need to get to the bottom of what is stopping them. It may be easier to take this 'off-line'. Other options are to appoint someone else to work with them on the task or ask someone else to take responsibility instead.

When people hold differing views about a topic you can sometimes find this leads to heated debate. This can result in thoughtless or even personal comments being made. When there is friction or even a full-scale argument you need to take immediate action. Defuse the situation by asking everyone to focus on the issues. By putting the problem back on the table you can steer clear of personality clashes. Get people to stick to the facts and encourage everyone to remain calm. Humour can sometimes help too.

If things get seriously out of hand, call for order. If this does not work, ask the disruptive person to leave, or if necessary adjourn the meeting to another date.

The power of summarising

Summaries are an extremely powerful tool when you are chairing a meeting. To do it well you need to listen carefully to what is being said, extract the key points, and repeat them clearly and concisely at the end of each agenda item. This ensures that everyone knows who is to do what by when. It is always a good idea to say you are summarising: 'Let me sum up the discussion so far...' or 'Let me make sure I have got this right'. This encourages people to pay attention.

It is particularly useful to summarise when there has been a disagreement, as it helps you regain control. Isolating contentious issues can make people realise they actually agree with one another – they had just lost track of the argument. It is surprising how often people can reach agreement, carry on talking, and end up disagreeing again. Summarising also helps when the discussion is going round in circles. By summarising the key issues you focus people's minds and get the discussion back on track.

 Exercise

Plan your approach to chairing the next meeting you are due to attend. If this is not usually your responsibility, volunteer to fill in from time to time. Review how it went at the end of every meeting and seek ways to improve the impact you make on the process.

Give a little helping hand

When you are a participant in a meeting and the Chair is not handling things too well, be prepared to give them a little helping hand. You can make an impact by assisting them in keeping things on track. If the meeting starts to drift or run over time, take more of a leader's role: 'We've already spent 40 minutes on the figures and it is important to devote time to...' or 'We are all aware of Peter's views on the topic and I'm sure you would agree that it would be useful to hear what Sarah has to say'. In a respectful way, you are becoming a mini Chair.

Tips for teleconferencing success

More and more meetings are now conducted by teleconferencing, especially in global companies or where the organisation you work for does business across a number of locations. It can be a challenge to make teleconferences effective, and it is easy as a participant to create a negative impression. It is hard to create a connection over the phone in large telephone-based meetings where you have not met everyone before. Yet there are some simple things you can do to make a positive impact.

If you are running the meeting, make sure everyone is sent an agenda well beforehand and make sure you are the first one on the line. If you are a participant, be on time and announce your name as you arrive. The same disciplines and common courtesies apply for teleconferencing as they do for meetings. Start the meeting on time even if some people have not yet arrived. This means switching off your BlackBerry, pager or mobile phone so there will be no distractions. The same goes for your Instant Messenger – mark it as 'busy', to avoid interruptions. Have a list of the people attending in front of you. Better still, draw a circle on a page and place each person's name around it as if they are sitting at a virtual table. This technique can help you keep track of who is there and who has not spoken for a while. You can use the information to invite them to share their views.

If you are chairing a teleconference, create a set of ground rules at the start to help everyone follow good practice. Establish a rule that people say who they are before they speak. Unless everyone knows each other's voices extremely well, it can be confusing if you do not do this. For regular or frequent meetings with the same group of people, it can be helpful to revisit the rules at the start of every meeting.

One of the most challenging aspects of this type of meeting is the lack of visual cues to let you know when someone wants to speak. Do not worry too much if you interrupt someone who has paused rather than finished speaking, because people understand how hard it is to tell when they are done. The occasional interruption adds some much needed spark to the proceedings.

Avoid speakerphones

Do not be tempted to use a speakerphone when there are a few people in one location. It is a little like having a side conversation in an ordinary meeting – rude, and very distracting for others. The temptation will be strong to press the mute button and get on with other things. You would never do that in an ordinary meeting and it is just as bad in a phone meeting.

When you ban the mute button and the speakerphone it forces you to give your complete attention to what is happening in the meeting. If you do not do that, it is not really like having a meeting at all. It might as well be a briefing or a download of information. Meetings require interaction and that means being fully present.

Focus on the job

Focus your attention completely on the conversation. Using a headset can help with this and it makes it easier to make notes. Closing your eyes is effective, too, because it helps you to avoid distractions when you are listening to someone.

Some people are tempted to check their emails or something similar when they are on a teleconference call, and you can hear them rustling papers and tapping away on their keyboard. Don't do it. People find it off-putting, disrespectful and irritating.

Do your best to stick to the topic and note down who has agreed to do what. While these are standard requirements in an ordinary meeting, they become even more crucial with telephone meetings when it is easy to mis-hear or misunderstand. Ask people to repeat themselves if you are not sure. Do not do this too often, though, because it can be annoying to others and may reduce your impact – they are likely to assume you have not been listening or are doing something else in the background.

I hear you loud and clear

Try to speak slightly more slowly than usual, with an emphasis on clarity. Anyone who has had to listen to someone over a speaker-phone knows that clear speech can often fall by the wayside. So that you do not have to repeat yourself and waste valuable meeting time, make an extra effort to speak loudly, slowly and clearly. Refer back to Chapter 8 if you need a reminder of how to create an impact with your voice. This becomes even more important in teleconferencing.

 Exercise

Think back to your last teleconference. Choose two or more ways from the tips above to increase your impact.

Bring on the meetings

While meetings have a bad reputation among many business people, when you get them right you have a great chance of raising your profile. Learning to make the most of these opportunities is invaluable when it comes to making an impact. It is also simple to achieve and allows you to stand out as an example of excellence.

Make an impact now

- Start creating a plan for how you will make a positive impact at your next meeting.
- Volunteer to chair a meeting so you can showcase your leadership skills.
- When an opportunity arises, put forward a clear, concise, coherent case for something important to you.

Chapter 12

Emailing with impact and more

'Those who write clearly have readers,
those who write obscurely have
commentators.'

Albert Camus

They say you can't judge a book by its cover. But you can certainly judge someone by their emails – and most of us do. We hear the 'you've got mail' ping, open up the message and within a couple of seconds of reading it we have formed an impression of the other person.

If the email seems to be 'all over the place', and we struggle to extract the message, we are likely to get annoyed and form a negative impression. If it is well-written and well-organised, and we can deal with it quickly and efficiently, we probably have a positive impression.

These days, often the first contact we have with someone is via email. In fact, sometimes we never speak to them at all or meet them face to face. The entire relationship is virtual, conducted through the screen of a computer or mobile phone.

Virtual impact

What does that mean for the impact you make? Well, since people can't see or hear you, body language and voice play no part. The impression they have of you is entirely down to the words you write and how well they represent your thoughts.

Some people are good at writing emails. If anything, they find it easier than having to present their ideas in person. They can take the time to craft them so they express their ideas as perfectly as possible.

Most of us, though, are very, very, *very* busy. We dash off emails as quickly as we can, simply to keep pace with a seemingly relentless stream of them filling up our inbox. We don't have time to agonise over whether to use this adjective or that verb. We just want to get them sent.

And there is the problem. When we do anything quickly we are prone to do it badly. Which can have devastating consequences for the impression others have of us.

What about the emails you receive?

Chances are you receive dozens of emails a day – maybe even more. Take a moment to reflect on what it is about them that gives you a positive or negative impression of the sender.

What did you come up with? Most people focus on problems with emails. They want to be able to open their inbox and crunch through the messages as efficiently as possible. Anything that gets in the way of that is perceived negatively – along with the person who sent the email. Typical complaints include:

- Missing/ambiguous/old subject line
- Purpose or message unclear
- Spelling/punctuation/grammar mistakes
- Too much content/detail/information
- No salutation or sign-off
- Tone unfriendly or even aggressive

Five secrets to maximising your email impact

It goes without saying, therefore, that you should avoid such things. If you don't like them, the same will be true of others. Let us take a look at five secrets to maximise your email impact.

1 Avoid silly mistakes

You open up an email and in the first paragraph – just 25 words – you spot a couple of errors. There is an apostrophe missing and one of the words is spelt wrongly. What is your impression of the sender? Careless? Lazy? Clueless? How much confidence do you have in the content?

It is not a big deal if you are emailing a friend, but mistakes in business communications are toxic. Even a single slip-up can raise doubts about the accuracy of the rest of the document. Your credibility is destroyed. As the business guru Tom Peters says, 'Coffee stains on the fold-down tray of an aircraft mean the company doesn't do its engine maintenance carefully.'

Many people are pedantic. If you are one of them, you will need no urging to avoid mistakes. It will be second nature. If you are not bothered by errors, you might think it does not matter. But it does matter. People who care about getting things right care *a lot*. Your document needs to be accurate or they will judge you negatively.

So use the spell check – *every* time – not just for 'special' or 'important' messages. Then read from start to finish, looking for errors it has missed, including punctuation and grammar. Automated programs are never foolproof. You need to check yourself to make sure.

What should you look for? The most common problems are:

- Missing words – just not there.
- Replacement words – eg. 'if' for 'is' or 'of'.
- The wrong word – eg. 'infer' instead of 'imply'.
- Apostrophes in plurals – 'file's' when it should be 'files'.
- Missing apostrophes in possessives – eg. 'Jacks book' when it should be 'Jack's book'.
- Poor grammar – eg. 'Jack and myself went to the meeting' instead of 'Jack and I went to the meeting'.

2 Be clear, concise and coherent

Most people don't have time to read long emails – and will have a positive impression of you if you get to the point, delivering your message clearly and concisely. Send them dense and detailed emails, on the other hand, and they may end up frustrated and annoyed with you for wasting their precious time.

So be clear. Say it straight. Use simple, everyday words and phrases. Avoid pompous, pretentious language. Just a few subtle changes can make a world of difference – the difference between stuffy, old-fashioned correspondence and modern business communication.

Avoid: *In relation to the aforesaid documents which make reference to…*

Use: *The documents we have highlighted refer to…*

Avoid: *Our solution has been designed in such a fashion as to adhere to the obligations and requirements of regulatory bodies…*

Use: *In designing the solution we have complied with regulatory requirements….*

Keep messages as brief as possible. If your email is too long, people will read the first and last paragraphs and skim read the middle, potentially missing important information. Follow the mantra 'less is more' and you won't go far wrong. Make every word count. Avoid waffle. What you are trying to say should be immediately obvious. Do not make the reader work hard to figure it out.

You also need to make sure your message is coherent. If there is no logical flow, with one thought leading naturally to the next – it seems 'all over the place' – you will irritate many readers. Group all comments on a particular topic together. Plan carefully to have maximum impact.

3 Make it readable

What is your reaction when you open up an email and see a solid block of text? If you are like most people, you'll find it impenetrable and unappealing and you won't feel much like reading it.

High impact emails are easy to read and easy to understand. So you need to break up longer chunks of text. There are several ways of doing that, some of which you probably use already. The most common are paragraphs, bullet points and sub-headings.

Paragraphs

If you were taught about paragraphs at school you were probably told that each one should contain a single idea – and this is still a solid principle to follow. But you may have to 'force' the break to stop the email becoming unreadable. Keep most paragraphs to below four lines, so the reader's eye skips over them quickly, and avoid going above six lines unless there's a good reason.

Bullet points

One of the best ways of breaking up an email is to use bullet points. They should be the first thing you think of whenever you have a list of things to cover. Using bullets to separate them out opens up the page and makes it more readable.

Sub-headings

Many people use sub-headings in reports, proposals and other kinds of writing, but never think of using them in emails. They work extremely well when you have several items to cover and you want to make the content accessible. Your impact is positive because the email has a clear structure, is well laid out and easy to read.

4 Remember the human

In the rush to clear your inbox it can be all too easy to forget that living, breathing human beings will be receiving your messages.

> think very carefully about what your reaction would be to your own email

The detached nature of the medium can also lead you to say things you would not say over the phone or face to face. So think very carefully about what your reaction would be to your own email.

It used to be easy. For many years there were clear rules about how to communicate in writing – established conventions that you followed if you wanted to make a positive impression.

You'd start a letter Dear Sir or Dear Madam and end with Yours Faithfully if you knew them and Yours Sincerely if you didn't. With email, though, there are no rules – and that makes life difficult.

Certainly you should be friendly and courteous. In a business email you should be professional. But getting the tone right can be tricky, and this is where there is sometimes an impact problem. Sometimes you need to be formal, sometimes friendly and occasionally familiar. Let us look at each in turn.

Formal writing tends to:

- employ more sophisticated words
- avoid contractions (uses 'we are' rather than 'we're')
- use a more complex sentence structure
- have no personal pronouns ('the company' rather than 'we').

Familiar writing tends to:

- use simpler words
- contract words using apostrophes ('you're' rather than 'you are')
- have a straightforward sentence structure
- include slang words and colloquialisms
- use personal pronouns ('We' and 'I').

Friendly writing ...

● is somewhere in-between – neither at one extreme nor the other.

Look at the following examples:

● **Formal**: Our research facility, introduced at the end of last year, has enjoyed a favourable response.

● **Friendly**: Our new research department is proving really popular with clients who use it.

● **Familiar**: We're chuffed to see the research dept going down a bomb.

Choosing your style

To make the right impact, you need to get the tone right. Generally you will want to be **friendly** in an email. **Familiar** language can be used in emails when you know people very well – but you should be careful in a work context. Certainly you should never use text speak – gr8 2 hr frm u – in a business email.

Salutations and sign-offs

Something many people find challenging is knowing how to start an email. 'Hi' is the commonest salutation, especially where you have established some kind of relationship.

'Dear' is common in some areas of business and less likely to offend in the early stages of a relationship or when you are emailing someone for the first time. 'Good morning/afternoon' are reliable standbys, as is 'Hello'.

If you are replying to an email sent to you, see what the other person chose and, all things being equal, use that.

The worst thing you can do is have no salutation at all. You just start your message. Many people find this extremely rude and curt – and it can leave them with a really negative impression. The only exception is when you swap a string of messages with someone, and saying 'Hi' every time would seem as unnatural as shaking hands every time you chatted with them on the same day.

Sign-offs

There are various ways of signing off. 'Best Regards' is acceptable to most business people, as is a simple 'Regards'. 'Best Wishes' is also popular with friends and family but in business people often dislike it as it reminds them of birthday cards. If the other person has done something for you, consider 'Thanks' as a sign-off. Some people are now using 'Thanks and regards'.

If you know the person, something more informal, such as 'Cheers', can be okay. Take care with expressions such as 'Warm Regards' and 'Warmest Wishes'. Some professionals find them 'wishy-washy' for business use – like having a weak handshake. Having no sign-off is off-putting to some people, because it suggests you're more interested in the task than the person.

5 Get the technical side of emailing right

While getting the content and tone of an email right can be tricky, there is no excuse for messing up the technical side. There are simple things you need to do if you are to be effective and make a positive impact.

Put the bottom line in the subject line

Make it clear from the 'Subject' line of the email what the message is about. Don't be clever and don't be cryptic. And don't just leave the heading the same as it was when you received it by hitting 'Reply' and having a 'Re:' followed by what was there when you received the email unless the content of your reply matches the header precisely. That's very lazy. Choose a clear, simple subject line that reflects the content of the email.

Poor: Boxing day
Good: The deadline for the box dimensions is Thursday

Poor: Meeting time
Good: 2.30pm is perfect for the strategy meeting

Deadlines need headlines

When you are requesting action or information by a particular date, make sure the person you are emailing can't miss that fact. Put a message such as 'Urgent – Immediate Action Required' either in the subject line or right at the beginning of the message. Do not put it in the middle or leave it to the end, where it might get missed. And be sure to clarify who or what the deadline refers to.

One subject, one email

Whenever possible, avoid raising loads of issues or answering lots of questions in one email. Consider sending two or more separate emails to minimise the risk of important information being missed. Lengthy emails can be hard to read when using devices that have small screens, such as BlackBerrys and iPhones.

Having different emails for each subject also helps to keep your emails short – which, as we observed earlier, means they are more likely to get read and have greater impact. It also enables you and your recipients to group emails into their topics so it's easier to track a conversation.

Say first things first

In most cases you will want to put the most important thing you have to say first. People are busy, get dozens – sometimes hundreds – of emails, and often do not have the patience to plough through your message to find out what you're saying. Your most important statements should appear in the first paragraph. Follow up with a succession of supporting details.

Other writing

Many business people have to write other documents at work – reports, proposals, memos, letters, etc. – and much of the advice above applies to them as well. Such documents are sometimes circulated widely, and may be seen by senior people and colleagues outside your area. If they do not know you personally, they will form an impression of you on the basis of your writing alone, so it needs to be good.

Who's Googling you?

Actually it is not true to say that email is the first point of contact people have with you. Often people will have 'Googled' you and looked at any profile you may have on the internet, including LinkedIn, Ecademy and Facebook.

Your web presence will make an impact. The question is, are you happy with the impact you're making? What would a prospective employer make of your profile? Would you be comfortable with anyone you hadn't met before seeing the pictures you have on Facebook? Does it fit with your personal 'brand' image? It's all too easy to make a bad impression or undersell your capability and end up being overlooked for opportunities that otherwise might come your way.

The internet provides a great vehicle for you to raise your profile. If you're not on LinkedIn or similar sites you may be missing an excellent opportunity to connect to a wide range of people. There are many groups you can join too.

If you are already signed up for these sites take a long hard look at your profile. Do you really present yourself in the way that you want? What can you do to make your entry more compelling? Who might give you a recommendation? Make sure you include a picture (and it is professional-looking), your job title (which is up to date) and a headline that sells the value you offer. If you have a website make sure it is listed. A strong summary helps people get a feel for what you are like and have to offer. Check for spelling and grammar errors too!

Make an instant impact

Instant messages are also part of our lives. Whether you are at work or at home, online chat is one of the key ways people communicate at a distance. It is also a minefield for the uninitiated of how easily you can reduce your impact. Take a look at our list of top ten toxic traits and discover how to avoid the 'horns effect'.

Top ten toxic traits for online messaging

1 Many people find instant messages intrusive – especially at work. Be respectful of their time and circumstances.

2 Sending messages when the other person is set to 'appear offline' or 'away' can irritate the recipient as they see the message pop up on the screen. Either wait until they are online or, if it's urgent, call and leave a voicemail.

3 Saying *Hi, how are you?* and then waiting for a reply before getting to the point you want to make. While this is less important among family and friends, at work many people find it annoying and time-wasting.

4 A lot of people use abbreviations and 'text speak' when chatting online. While this is fine among friends it does reduce your impact at work. It is not considered professional. Take the time to use capital I rather than lower case and avoid LOL or other similar acronyms.

5 ☺ Smileys! People love them or hate them. The secret here is to only use them with people who send them to you and never, never use them at work.

6 Leaving long delays before replying or starting to write and then stopping are often quoted in the top ten hates list of instant messaging. Keep it quick and simple.

7 Long drawn-out messages that take an age to write. If you want to discuss something in detail pick up the telephone instead.

8 An abrupt end with no sign-off. Take the time to say goodbye before you rush off to do something else rather than leaving the other person wondering where you went.

9 Writing in a sloppy or careless fashion. Be aware that some people save what you write and you never know where it will turn up!

10 Approaching people you have never met before without an introduction. Don't send a message to people you don't know – for many people it is spam.

Make an impact now

- Take a look at your sent box and review your emails – how can you make a better impact?

- Get feedback from a friend or colleague who has good attention to detail and writes well.

- Google yourself and see what comes up. Examine your online profiles and find ways to improve the impression you make.

Chapter 13

Get the job you want – then get a raise

'Being ready isn't enough; you have to be prepared for a promotion or any other significant change.'

Pat Riley, leading American basketball coach

Y ou have arrived 15 minutes early as planned and are now waiting to go into your job interview. The receptionist has gone to get you a glass of water. This is always the worst bit. Waiting seems to make you even more nervous. Will they want to know about that gap in your CV? What if they ask a really tough question you have not thought about? What if you have not got the right level of experience? You have been practising all week – going over and over various answers in your mind. You are desperate to make the right impact and get this job.

Be confident from the start

In the days leading up to an interview it is normal to feel anxious – especially when you really, really want the position. Preparation can help a lot. If you have thought about the questions you may get asked and have planned various possible responses, you will start to feel more comfortable. When you are confident, you come across with more impact. Remembering times when you success- fully handled similar situations in the past will also help. The memory will evoke the feelings of success and re-experiencing them improves your state so you feel better able to handle an interview. Take deep breaths to calm you down before you go in. Above all, believe in yourself and what you have to offer. A positive and enthusiastic attitude goes a long way towards making an impact in an interview.

The person you spoke to on the phone last week, Dawn, walks into reception to greet you. She smiles and asks you about your journey. Already you start to feel more at ease. You remember the importance of first impressions and smile as you shake hands. She guides you down a long corridor to a room at the rear of the building and asks you to take a seat. You feel good about the clothes you are wearing – just as well you decided to check what the dress code was likely to be. You are also relieved that you opted for your favourite blue suit and white shirt; it not only looks good but also feels comfortable to wear.

Make a fantastic first impression

The first seven seconds of an interview can mean success or failure. Research shows that people rarely change their view afterwards, no matter how qualified you are for the role, so the impact you make at the outset is crucial for your success. There are certain things you must avoid at all costs, because many interviewers have a problem with them, including:

- being late with no good reason
- wearing too much perfume or aftershave
- carrying shopping you bought on your way
- wearing clothes that are dishevelled
- ostentatious jewellery and accessories.

You are not just looking to make a positive first impression on the person who will be interviewing you. Be friendly with receptionists, PAs and everyone you meet, too, as staff members are sometimes asked to chip in with their views. Apply all the suggestions we made in Chapter 3 on how to make a great first impression and you will not go far wrong.

Dawn says a colleague will be joining her for the first interview, then you will be asked to complete some personality/psychometric tests, and finally you will have a meeting with someone you would be working alongside if you get the job and who will be part of the decision-making process.

Interview formats

Some interviews are just with one or two people, one of whom is usually your prospective line manager. Others take place before a panel made up of several people. Each person on the panel may have a specific role to play – but not always. One may be the line manager, another from HR, and so on. There is usually one person who asks most of the questions. Panel interviews can feel intimidating but in some ways they are the same as a one-to-one interview. When you arrive be sure to make eye contact with everyone and smile. Focus most of your attention on the person who asks the questions, while periodically looking at the others on the panel.

An alternative structure some companies adopt is to have a series of meetings on the same day, one after another. This can be tiring so the important thing is to maintain your energy. Greet each person you meet as if they are the first interviewer of the day.

Did your phone manner hit the mark?

Some companies like to conduct a telephone interview before meeting you face to face. These are either formal interviews or they call without warning and it is more like an informal chat. Don't be fooled by this. You are being evaluated all the time. Creating the right impression over the phone is crucial, especially when the job involves a lot of telephone work.

It could, of course, be the other way round. You call them for more information – perhaps to ask for a job description. This can go down really well because not many people bother to make a personal connection beforehand. But, once again, the impression they have of you during this call will form part of their decision-making process.

If you went through a recruitment agency

If you went through a recruitment agency you will have been through a screening process. This often includes a face-to-face interview which can help you to prepare for the real thing. It is important to remember that you need to create a positive impression when you meet agency staff because they will help to sell you to their clients.

Dawn and her colleague James start by explaining the process they will follow: some general questions first, then a few about your CV, followed by some discussion about what the company is looking for and then there will be time for you to ask questions. You already know there will be some psychometric tests and a personality questionnaire afterwards, plus the meeting with the person you might work alongside. The letter said the whole process may last around an hour and a half. Dawn kicks off with her first question: 'Tell me about yourself.' You have heard that people often start with broad questions like this to help people relax – but how do you answer them with impact?

Answering questions

Really broad questions like this can wrong-foot you. Do you tell them about you and your life in general? If you are not sure what they are after, it is best to ask a question to clarify. If you choose to answer from a work context, they will soon let you know if they want to know more about you as a person. What is most important is to answer in an upbeat and positive way. Imagine how you would feel if someone said 'Well my life is a bit humdrum really. [Long pause, giving the impression you have no idea what to say next.] I suppose I like reading and spending time with my friends.' It is hardly a high-impact response is it? Try this instead: 'I love being busy and having plenty to do at work. I like working as part of a team. [Short pause.] Outside work I enjoy spending time on a mixture of things.'

The questions keep coming. 'What do you enjoy most about your current job?' 'Which aspect don't you like and why?' 'What do you know about our company?' 'Why do you think you would be right for the job?' Gradually the questions will start to get trickier.

What is crucial before any interview is to anticipate the questions you are likely to be asked. Some of them will be fairly standard and based around your existing experience. The ones most people do not like answering are when they invite you to say something negative about yourself. The best way to deal with these is to be honest but put a positive spin on your answer. 'When I first started the job I did not enjoy filing much but I have learnt how valuable it is to have everything in the right place so other people can find things when they need to.' If filing is a central part of the job you are applying for, they will at least feel you understand why it is important. The answer also demonstrates your ability to learn. It is a good idea to choose something like filing, which people often associate with being a bit tedious.

When you are preparing for an interview, you need to do your homework. The bare minimum is to look at the company's website. You would be amazed how many people do not bother to do this, so it immediately makes you look switched on. If you know someone who works for the company, you can also get inside information on the culture.

If you have not seen a detailed job description, and the advertise-ment is a bit skimpy, you will need to know more about what the job entails. Before you can answer questions such as 'Why do you think you would be right for the job?', you will need to know a bit more about the role. Some interviewers will give you a quick overview within the first 15 minutes. If they do not, ask them to bring the job to life for you first.

Competencies and the STAR model

Interviewers vary enormously in how prepared they are, how structured they are – and, frankly, how good they are. Some are 'all over the place': jumping from one thing to another, with no clear order and no clear objective. Others – especially those from leading companies – use a structured approach based on behavioural competencies to assess your suitability for the role, such as communication, self-motivation, teamwork, planning and customer service. The job advertisement often provides clues to what the competencies are. You could also phone and ask if they can send you a more detailed job description.

These companies often use the STAR format for probing on competencies:

Situation – this is the situation where you used/demonstrated the competence

Task – the task you had to complete

Action – the actions you took

Result – the results of those actions

It is considered a fair and objective approach to interviewing because they ask every candidate the same structured questions. If you have got a good idea of what the competencies are, you can brainstorm answers that follow this approach in advance.

For example, let us assume that the competency the interviewer wants to explore is communication. They will have several questions prepared that are tailored for the role you are applying for, such as:

1 Tell me about a situation where you had to obtain information to better understand a customer's needs.

2 Describe a challenging situation you have handled while dealing with a customer complaint and how you approached it.

What they are seeking to do is to uncover background information about the context and situation, the part you played in the task, the actions you personally took and the outcome of those actions. The interviewer asks probing follow-on questions until they have the full picture of what happened.

In answer to Question 1 you might say: 'I consider it important to fully understand what all my customers want. A specific example of this happened only a month ago. I went to see Ryan at Marble Glass. He buys a lot of our products and the orders have dropped off recently. I asked him how things were going and he told me that one of their major suppliers had let them down and he had been busy trying to find an alternative. I spent some while listening to him talk about his issues and asking questions to get a full understanding. I found a way to help him by putting him in touch with someone I know who does what he is looking for. Last week he booked another order twice the size of the previous ones.'

For Question 2 your answer might be something like: 'It may sound strange but I enjoy the challenge of dealing with difficult situations. It gives me a sense of satisfaction when I turn them round. The production team had severe staff shortages which meant they got behind. Clare at Credence was not happy – angry would be a better description – and understandably so. I let her get her feelings out of her system and apologised unreservedly for our mistake. I find it takes the steam out of situations like this when you agree with them rather than getting defensive. I arranged for her order to be priori-tised and sent her some flowers. Clare loves lilies. I phoned the next day to check the order had turned up on time.'

If the example you want to use is based around something you did as part of a team, make the part you played in it clear. They want to find out about the impact you made *personally*. The STAR model framework gives you a great opportunity to demonstrate all the ways you make an impact already.

10 top tips for making an impact with your answers

1 Make your answers clear, concise, coherent and compelling.

2 Be honest – it is all too easy to get found out if you elaborate on the truth.

3 Explain precisely what part you played when describing achievements.

4 Choose a task that is reasonably challenging rather than humdrum.

5 Just like an exam – make sure you answer the question they ask.

6 Do not memorise your answers word for word or you will sound stilted.

7 Make sure your answers are relevant to the job you are applying for.

8 Stay calm and listen carefully to each question.

9 Ask the interviewer to explain or repeat a question if you do not understand.

10 Be enthusiastic about the results of your actions.

 Exercise

Create a list of competencies for your current job. Bring each one to life with impact – as if to an interviewer – following the STAR method.

Dawn picks up your CV and starts to ask some questions about it. There are several areas where she would like more information – and a couple of inconsistencies she would like to iron out.

Making sure your CV has impact

Experienced interviewers spend less than two minutes reading a CV, so you have a real challenge to make an impact that differentiates your CV from the stack on their desk. Interviewers are looking to see if there is a fit in terms of your knowledge, skills, experience, capabilities and attitude. 'Fit' is an important word to a seasoned recruiter; they are practised in the art of skimming CVs and comparing them with the job requirements. An awful lot of candidates fall at this hurdle because they create a one-size-fits-all résumé. If you have got as far as the interview it is likely that you have already succeeded with your CV – at least to some extent. The questioning process allows them to dig deeper and find out just how good a fit it really is.

One of the most common mistakes people make with CVs is that they do not tailor the content for each job they apply for. It is worth the effort to do this because it increases the odds of getting that all-important interview no end. The advertisement or job description will give you plenty of clues about what they want. Here are some things to bear in mind if you want to improve your chances of getting to the interview stage:

1 **Spelling and grammar**: Number one on the list is poor spelling and grammar. The impression is if you cannot make the effort on a CV you will be even worse when you get the job. Spell-check it as a minimum and get someone else to read it through as an added safeguard.

2 **Clear structure and format**: Keep it simple and succinct. Make sure facts and dates are correct. Use the same font throughout, do not use underlining and do have lots of white space. There are plenty of good books on the market that tell you how to lay out your CV. It should usually include a career statement (what you are looking for from a job) your name, education details, work history and references. Jim Bright and Joanne Earl in their book *Brilliant CV* say that including competency statements increases your chances of getting an interview by 30 per cent. This is a list of attributes such as team work, communication and problem-solving, with a short description that demonstrates your abilities in each one.

3 **Don't be modest**: Resist the temptation to be too modest, but keep it real. Include all your achievements, such as Employee of the Month Award, exceeding sales targets and winning promotion; all too often people leave them out or play them down. If you have been involved in a project, make the outcome clear, because people look to see if you complete things. Use positive, strong words such as 'overcame', 'achieved', 'created', 'completed', 'organised' and 'accomplished'.

4 **Turn negative points into positives**: If you think something on your CV could be considered a negative, turn it into a positive or leave it out altogether. Many recruiters look for continuity of employment; demonstrating steady progress up the career ladder is even better. If you have any gaps between jobs explain them briefly – 'During my year out I developed my leadership skills by working with disabled children.'

5 **Covering letters count**: Covering letters are a great opportunity to sell yourself and your enthusiasm for the job. Keep the tone positive and limit yourself to one page. Make sure the letter is tailored for the job you're applying for. If you send your letter and CV by email, make the subject line clear and read through it for mistakes before you hit 'send'.

 Exercise

Review your current CV and compare it with the points we have outlined above. Improve it generally and then tailor a version for a job you have in mind for your next career step.

As the interview progresses, James becomes more active – and slightly more aggressive. Are they running some kind of good cop/bad cop routine? Some of his questions are extremely challenging.

Always expect the unexpected

It is important to prepare for questions and anticipate tough ones you may be asked. There are lots of good books around that contain examples of the most challenging questions that get asked, such as 'Do you consider yourself to be a leader or a follower?' or 'What sort of things do you and your current boss disagree about?' Some people ask them to see how you react under pressure.

Questions like these provide you with a great opportunity to make a positive impact. Let us take the first example. How you answer this depends, to some extent, on the role you are applying for. If the job involves managing a team, the question is potentially provocative. The most important thing here is to remain calm and not take it as personal criticism. Obviously you are going to opt for leader, but you need to back up that claim with evidence. Pick a good example that demonstrates your leadership skills. If the role does not require you to manage others, let them know that you are comfortable in either role, especially if you are looking for promotion in the future. Once again, back this up with proof in the shape of an example. You could even add that you look forward to the time when you will be able to manage a team in the future.

When people ask you questions about your current boss they are probably testing to find out what you will be like to manage. This gives you the chance to show that you can take instruction and are assertive enough to share your views. End each example with a positive result, even if the reason you are leaving is because you do not get on with your boss. Because interviewers do not know the full story, they may assume that some of the problems lie with you.

Having completed the first part of the interview Dawn smiles and says, 'Right, over to you. What questions would you like to ask?' Phew! Nearly at the end. But you realise that this section is just as important as the rest and may influence the outcome.

Your chance to give them a grilling

There is nothing worse than getting to the point where it is your turn to ask questions and not being able to think of anything to say. It happens more often than you might think – especially when people are new to the whole job-hunting process. You need to put effort into preparing questions to ask at this stage of the interview. Remember, it is a two-way process, so do not be afraid to ask challenging or detailed questions about the role and the organisation.

The interviewer will be impressed that you care enough to find out whether the job is right for you; they do not want to take someone on only to have them leave after a few weeks. You can ask about the team, company culture, business priorities and the markets in which the organisation operates. You may have questions about the role – such as why the position is available, if it is possible to meet the team you will be working with and what will be expected of you in the first few months. Ask questions such as 'Tell me more about the company', or 'What opportunities are there for me to progress within the company?' Make it plain that you are interviewing them as much as they are interviewing you. If you seem desperate, you lower your perceived value.

Exit with impact

When the meeting is over it is easy to be tempted to relax. Big mistake. You are still on show all the time that you are in the building. Maintain your energy and enthusiasm – even if you are feeling a bit tired, remember this is the last chance you will have to make a positive impact on them. Ask them what happens next, if they have not already made this clear. Thank the interviewer, smile and shake their hand if they go to shake yours. Say something positive such as 'I look forward to hearing from you next week.'

Psychometric tests and assessment centres

Many organisations use psychometric tests and personality questionnaires as part of the recruitment process. You can buy books that give you advice on how to complete them, including sample questions to practise. Verbal and numerical critical reasoning tests are carried out in timed, exam-like conditions. Make sure you:

- read the instructions carefully
- ask for clarification if you do not understand something
- work as quickly and accurately as possible
- miss out any questions you get stuck on
- record your answers in the right boxes.

There are many different types of personality questionnaires for which there are no right or wrong answers; there is not much you can do in terms of making an impact with them. The best policy is to be honest. These tests are used to get a better understanding of you as a person and to help the interviewers decide whether there is a fit with the role.

Some companies use assessment centres – this is very common in graduate recruitment and leadership profiling. You will take part in a series of exercises that test your abilities against defined behavioural competencies. The activities vary and include: in-tray exercises, case studies, and team or communication exercises.

Think about what they are likely to be measuring in each activity. Aim to demonstrate your strengths by actively participating in each task. How you respond in role-plays and team exercises makes a big impact. This can be positive or negative: it will reveal how you relate to others, whether or not you take control, how creatively you approach the task, and so on.

Don't be a shrinking violet. Join in and put forward your views. The assessors are often looking to see how you go about the task rather than whether you end up with the right answers. Equally, don't treat it like an opportunity to beat everyone else there and take over the proceedings too much. They nearly always want people who can work together effectively.

The second or third (or fourth!) interview

Well done if you are invited back for a second, third or even fourth interview. This means you have made it to the shortlist. Although four interviews are pretty unusual, don't fall into the trap of showing your impatience. The interviewers' intention is to be sure they have the right person for the role. This is a real opportunity to convince them they should choose you above the rest.

You sometimes find this interview is with someone more senior, so expect the questions to be broader in nature. They may ask you about your plans for the next five years or how you feel you can add value to the company. You may also find they ask you the same questions you were asked first time round. What is crucial is to answer as if you have been asked the question for the first time. This keeps your energy high and it also gives you a chance to improve on the way you expressed yourself the first time.

Towards the end of the interview, when it is your turn for questions, uncover any potential unspoken objections. 'Is there anything about me you are not sure about that needs further clarification?' If there is any doubt in their mind, they will let you know and you have a chance to deal with it. If not, they will admire you for being bold enough to ask.

The job's yours!

Waiting to hear can be a tense time. If this period drags on and you have not heard for over a week, it is a good idea to get in touch – it shows you are keen. You also need to be respectful that they may have good reasons for delaying telling you whether or not you have been successful.

Getting yourself promoted

If you want to be promoted you need to manage the impact you create on an ongoing basis way before the time you apply for promotion. The impression you make in meetings, presentations and conferences all count. Your reputation is likely to go before you. Even in a large organisation people often know people who know you. Common sense says they will ask questions about you if you apply for a role in their area.

Internal vacancies are often advertised openly so that anyone with the right skills and experience can apply. Do not rely on this alone. Many people secure jobs through their network of personal contacts within an organisation. If you have been actively raising your profile and making a positive impact, as we recommended in Chapter 1, this should be fairly simple. Let people know that you are looking for a move. You never know what is out there until you start spreading the word.

Be realistic and ask yourself whether you are actually ready for a promotion. If you end up struggling in a new role you will find it hard to create impact as quickly as you want. Check out the competencies for the next role and work out which ones you need to improve. A higher-level job should provide a stretch. If you had all of the skills already it would not be worth going for it anyway. Find opportunities to demonstrate the capabilities you need in your current role – perhaps by taking on a special project. Manage your image. Get feedback on your impact from people you trust. Tell your boss where you want to be in two years' time and keep asking for feedback to find out whether you are on track.

You will need to tell your boss about your plans at some stage. You are likely to be the best judge of when, because much depends on your relationship. Do consider things from their point of view, though; if you leaving will make life difficult for them it can help to let them know early and work with them to create a plan to find your replacement. Some bosses will actively help you in your quest to find the right position. This can take the form of advice or simply 'oiling the wheels' through their contacts in different departments.

Ask for a raise – and get it

Many people never ask for a pay rise. Guess what? All they get is the annual inflation rise if they are lucky. The first step to getting a raise is to be bold. Let your boss know that is what you want. Women are reportedly much more reluctant than men to ask for what they want. You can't, of course, simply demand it and expect it to happen just like that; you need to prove you are worth it.

You will maximise your chances of success if you ask at the right time. Demonstrate you can achieve consistent top-quality results. Be assertive and respectful of their situation at the same time. Some organisations have policies on pay rises and HR has a say over when it happens and who gets one. Start by researching what is possible. Who else has got a raise? If you can, find out how much it was.

> demonstrate you can achieve consistent top-quality results

If the pay decision is out of your immediate boss's hands, you – or your boss on your behalf – may need to make your case to whoever makes the decision. Sometimes pay is determined by special committees, and this may mean putting something in writing to support your argument. Do some research on job advertisements posted on internet sites or by talking to friends in other companies to find out what the going rate is for the role. Find out who is involved in making the decision and manage your image with them. Take every opportunity to let people know about your achievements, without bragging.

You need a hook to persuade the decision-maker. It may be that you do a deal with them that you get the pay rise when you achieve your sales target for three months in a row. Be ready to negotiate if your boss says 'no'. It may be you think it is worth having an extra two days' holiday in lieu of pay or a company car.

Every step of the way

You will know when you are ready for a change, but keep an eye on what is out there. Be prepared to work on your impact on a daily basis to demonstrate your potential for the next step up the career ladder. Believe in yourself and your abilities. You never know when the job of your dreams is going to appear; if you are prepared, you can leap into action and raise that bar for yourself. In the meantime, review each aspect of the job-hunting process and make sure you create the best possible impact through your behaviour and attitude when the time is right for action.

Make an impact now

- Take a long hard look at your CV and then turn it into something that is guaranteed to get you interviews.
- Be positive about your experience and be prepared to sell your strengths to people inside and outside your organisation.
- Enlist a friend to help you rehearse answers to questions you may be asked at interview.
- Do some research to find out what the usual pay is for a role like yours so you are ready to take action and ask for more.

Chapter 14

Building your social and professional network

'The most potent people I've known have been the best networkers – they "know everybody from everywhere" and have just been out to lunch with most of them.'

Tom Peters, management guru

Are you on Facebook? With over 100 million active users, it is the fastest growing online social network in the world since its inception in February 2004. What is the attraction? People can catch up with long-lost friends, meet new people, communicate through messaging with individuals or groups, organise social occasions ... and a whole lot more. It's quick, it's easy, it's fun. It gets you exposure to masses of people in an instant.

People have a desire, an urge, to network – and not just online. They love to meet, greet and build relationships. We are social creatures and we want to be around others.

That is why one of the most effective ways of enhancing your impact is by establishing a large network of professional and social contacts. Business is personal. We prefer to work with people we know and like and trust – and networking is about making connections and growing your circle of influence. Whether you are a PA or whether you are a vice-president, you need people you are able to call upon as the need arises – people who will help you in a crisis, people who can give you information, people who can introduce you to other people.

You scratch my back ...

Why would they do that? Because they have the same need. They will do that for you – and you will do that for them. It is reciprocal.

It is 'you scratch my back and I will scratch yours'. It is all about building mutually beneficial relationships. It is not just a matter of you getting what you want; you help each other in a climate of support, trust and shared knowledge.

Some people feel uncomfortable about the idea of networking because it feels underhand, manipulative or sneaky to them. But that's only the case if you do it wrong. When it is done with the intention of making things better for everyone, it is a win–win process.

Some organisations now have networking as one of their competences – employees are expected to promote their workplace and pick up new contacts. Because of the fast pace of life, increased competition for business and the huge choice of products and services, many people are relying on networks to find information quickly and do business.

Business networks can be equally useful socially as well as professionally – trading information on great restaurants or where to buy the latest technology cheaply. Why waste time doing the research yourself when others can help – and give you personal recommendations?

Your network can be immensely useful in fast-tracking your career, solving problems, finding shortcuts and managing relationships. The more visible you are, the more impact you have.

Six degrees of separation

Have you heard of the six degrees of separation? This proven concept says it takes only six people to gain access to anyone in the world. Let us say you want to get to Madonna. Who do you know who might be on the edge of her world? Someone in the music business? A film maker? Someone who lives in her neighbourhood in London? You ask them to approach a contact in their network who talks to someone in their network, and so on until you finally get access to Madonna.

The research was originally based on participants given the challenge of locating a complete stranger on the other side of the USA. The task was to send the person a parcel. All they had was a name and the state. On average it took six mailings to find the person. This was repeated with emails years later and the number was confirmed. Because of technology, the latest research suggests that it now takes only 4.5 steps to get to anyone you want.

Once you are clear about your goals, leverage the networks you have and others too. The world is your oyster. Never underestimate the value of a contact: they may not be the person you directly want to target, but they may help you achieve the impact you want.

What are you trying to do?

Too many people decide they 'need to do more networking' but do not fully think through what they want to achieve. The more specific you are about your outcomes, the better. Taking a strategic approach is essential. Here are some of the issues to consider:

- What type of contacts do you want to make?
- Are you looking for prospects, clients, peers in similar organisations, decision-makers, experts, suppliers, new acquaintances, sporting partners or a travel companion?
- Is there anyone in particular – a named individual – you would like to get to know?
- Where do your networking targets go? How can you find out?
- How many new people do you want to meet?

Let's face it, you do not have time to build strong relationships with everyone you meet, so you need to be clear about what you want to achieve and have as much impact as possible when you do connect with others. The most important thing to understand is that quality is more important than quantity. You are busy; you cannot possibly maintain an enormous network, so you will need to be selective. In the 1800s the economist Vilfredo Pareto developed the 80:20 rule when he observed that 80 per cent of the wealth in Italy came from 20 per cent of the population. He developed the theory that 80 per cent of the effects come from 20 per cent of causes. Pareto's Law applies here: you will get 80 per cent of your benefit from 20 per cent of your contacts. So be selective, be focused.

Taking advantage of the 'hidden' job market

Many of the positions in organisations are never advertised. This is the 'hidden' job market. People are sometimes directly approached, or poached, as a result of reputation, referral or an existing relationship. That's why it is vital you raise your profile – they obviously will not come to you if they do not know you exist and have no idea what your skills and talents are. So you need to be visible, and get to know as many people as possible. The bigger your network, both internally and externally, the more likely you are to benefit from the hidden job market – rather than seeing a role you wanted being awarded to someone else without even knowing it was vacant.

It is the same if you work for yourself. Whether you are a gardener, wedding planner, hypnotherapist, plumber or consultant, you need customers or clients to find you – and word of mouth is the surest, safest way of building a business. Consummate networkers get work from people they meet on trains, at conferences, in restaurants, from breakfast clubs, at school events – and so on.

Be ready – anytime, anywhere

That is what makes great networkers successful – they are opportunistic. Like policemen, they are always 'on duty', always alert to the potential of meeting someone who could be useful. They connect with people wherever they are. The whole wide world is a 'room' to be worked.

It's only polite

A courtesy that many ignore is the RSVP. Whether you are planning to attend an event or you cannot make it, let the organisers know. It's considerate. Not doing so can make a negative impact. Many events are a big investment in time and money – you may not be the only person who has decided not to show. Your professional association or supplier may be a crucial contact in the future. Keep them on side. It only takes a moment to send an email or make a call.

Come on and 'work' that room

The most challenging part of networking, for most people, is striking up a conversation with strangers. You walk into a crowded reception at a conference – then what? Who do you talk to? How do you break into a group? What do you say? Almost everyone finds 'working a room' difficult.

Part of the problem is this notion of breaking into a group. It is an aggressive metaphor, and one which surely makes approaching others intimidating. You would not want to break into anyone's house, would you? Or their car? So why would you want to break into their group? What if you thought instead about joining a group? We like to join others for dinner. We like to join a book club or a wine circle. This is a friendly, collaborative act, not an aggressive one. How you think about what you are doing makes all the difference.

In practice you may never have to approach a group of strangers, since there will often be one person on their own – and few people find it hard to go up to individuals. If you are relatively quiet you might need to pluck up a little courage, but once you realise they feel the same, and will be delighted to speak to you, you can feel more comfortable and confident.

10 top tips for joining others with impact

1 **Avoid those you work with or already know**: Do not stick with the same old crowd – find potential new contacts to chat with.

2 **Target individuals first**: Most people find it easier to approach someone on their own – and they may be pleased to see you.

3 **Consider a group of three or more**: It can be relatively easy to join larger groups because they may have fragmented slightly.

4 **Avoid pairs/couples**: Only approach two people together if you have no choice or if it is obvious they are open to another person – heads close, leaning in, no gaps says 'do not go there'.

5 **Select the best group**: When there are several possible groups, consider those involved – who looks most likely to be on your wavelength?

6 **Don't be a stealth bomber**: Once you have chosen your group, do not hover on the edge or circle like a stealth bomber; approach confidently rather than tentatively.

7 **Choose the largest gap**: Do not push your way into a small gap. Choose the largest space to make your entrance.

8 **Catch someone's eye**: Normally someone will look at you as you join them. They will usually be listening rather than speaking. Catch their eye and they will turn to you.

9 **Ask 'May I join you?'**: It sounds like a question, and is respectful, but you are unlikely to get the answer 'No' unless there is a very good reason. Hold out your hand and introduce yourself.

10 **Go with the flow**: Do not take over the conversation. Either pick up on something that was being said or ask a question of the group.

Talk your way to success

While some people find it easy to chat effortlessly about pretty much anything under the sun, others struggle with small talk – and end up avoiding networking situations for fear of floundering after a few minutes. Lack of an effective strategy for starting and sustaining conversations holds them back. But actually it is relatively simple. When you use the OARS model described below – which is what those who are skilled at social networking do naturally – you will feel confident in your ability to keep things flowing.

Observe

Ask

Reveal

Share

Observe

Where do you start when you meet someone for the first time? One option that works well is to make an observation about the situation or environment you both find yourselves in. You might comment on the food, the location, or – if you had just heard someone speak – the presentation. A simple 'These canapés are great' or 'Isn't this building magnificent?' can be good icebreakers. If not, there is always that great British staple – the weather. To some extent it does not really matter what you say, because the purpose of the remark is only to open up the conversation. *How* you say it does matter though. The observations you make at the start need to be positive. If your opening comments are critical you will come across as negative, as a 'moaning minnie'. So do not say 'The canapés taste awful', even if they do, or 'This building has seen better days'.

Ask questions

The secret of being a successful conversationalist – whether you are networking or just chatting – lies in asking questions. Most people love to talk about themselves, so give them the chance. If you want others to think you are interesting, be interested.

Start with some broad, open questions, such as 'How do you like to spend your time?' This gives them the opportunity to discuss whatever they want. They might say 'I love to travel', or 'I'm into charity fundraising' – or even 'I work in marketing'. Ask them 'What hobbies do you have?' or 'What line of business are you in?' and you narrow their choice.

When they answer, listen carefully. Be a 'word detective', looking for leads that will guide you to the next question. What could you ask if someone said 'I love to travel'? There are many, many options. 'Have you been anywhere recently?', 'Do you have any trips planned?', 'What is your favourite place' – and so on. One question leads naturally to another. It is easy to keep going once you get started.

But how would it be for the other person if all you did was ask questions? It would feel like an interview – perhaps even an interrogation. That would make a negative impact, not a positive one.

Reveal

What you need to do is reveal something about yourself, so there is a sense of taking turns. Having asked three, maybe four, questions, you disclose some personal details. Not only are you making the conversation feel balanced, you are opening the door for other people to get to know you better. However, limit what you say about any particular topic, and avoid giving too much detail (unless others are really interested) or you will risk being labelled a bore.

Share

Most of the time when the conversation starts to flag you can lift it back up by asking another question. But it is also useful to have some 'bits' of information you can share with others. These might be amusing stories gleaned from the media, 'factoids' you have collected from the internet, or simply thoughts about what is happening in the world. To do this you need to have your antennae out, and keep up with the latest news. You would not dream of giving a presentation without preparing first – and it is the same with networking.

The OARS model in practice

You do not have to use OARS in a literal, linear fashion; the sequence can be fluid and free-flowing. Here are some examples of how it could work:

- 'This is the first time I have been to this event [R]. I thought the last speaker was particularly interesting [O]. What do you think? [A]'.

- 'I read an interesting article in the paper last week which contradicted what he said [S]. Would you be interested in hearing about it? [A]'.

- 'I was struck by what the speaker said about ... [O]. It's exactly what's happening in my organisation. [R]. What about yours? [A]'.

You also need to be careful about the kind of questions you ask. If they are too personal they may come across as intrusive.

Moving from small talk to big talk

Sometimes a social conversation is sufficient, but more typically you will want to shift gears and start talking about business – to find out if there is any mutual benefit. How do you go from small talk to big talk? Most of the time, it is just a matter of moving the discussion to a professional footing. People will often start talking about their work. If they don't, you could simply ask. A better alternative, though, is to reveal what you do – 'I am in retail' – and they are likely to reveal as well.

Introducing yourself effectively

Of course, you will know from experience that some people are more direct, and shortly after meeting you they will ask That Question: 'What do you do?' How do you respond? Do you have a crisp, clear answer? Or do you mumble something rather muddled about your industry, sector or job title? Most people do the latter – and seem surprised when the other person suddenly changes the subject.

Your personal introduction is one you will make over and over again, and it is a crucial part of your first impression. So it is worth sitting down and spending some time crafting it. It is important to be able to deliver it with confidence and conviction. In fact, you will need several different introductions, according to the situation and the person you are meeting. Time invested here is time rewarded.

Many books talk about having an 'elevator' pitch – so-called because you should be able to deliver it in the time it takes for an elevator to go from the bottom floor to the top. But an introduction of this kind can backfire. Many people are extremely sensitive to being sold to, especially in a networking situation, and will get suspicious if they sense you are acting solely out of self-interest. People want to spend time with people they like and they trust. If you 'pitch' to them too soon – or at all – you will set alarm bells ringing.

Hook, line and sinker

So go for an introduction that is more subtle. The best approach is to break it down into steps – and keep the first part short, but make it intriguing.

'So what do you do?'
'I help people change.'

Your aim should be to avoid them saying 'Oh, interesting …' and create a 'hook' that gets the other person to say 'How do you do that?' or 'Tell me more about that' – effectively inviting you to continue pitching to them.

'So what do you do?'
'I help people change.'
'How do you do that?'
'I'm a coach and a trainer.'

Another example:

'So what do you do?'
'I work with companies to minimise what they pay the government.'
'How do you do that?'
'I work in the taxation department of a Big Four accountancy firm.'

Some people will find it easier to do this than others. If you are a PA you could say 'I make sure the office runs smoothly' – but if you are with other PAs they will not be impressed. Most people though, with a little imagination, can produce a suitable hook. Here are some criteria:

- Keep it brief.
- Do not include too much detail.
- Aim to make it tabloid rather than broadsheet.
- Orient it round a potential benefit.

It's story time

If you get this right – the hook and the benefit – you may have the opportunity to expand on your introduction. You goal is to give an answer which encourages them to want to know more. The best way to continue is by telling a story. This should have a number of elements:

- what the challenge/problem is
- how you overcame it (skill, knowledge, experience)
- why the outcome was positive.

For example: 'I am just winding up a project with a client where we've saved £500,000 in tax benefits by helping them interpret new legislation. It was tricky negotiating with the government, but we're extremely experienced in this field and knew exactly which levers to pull – and we got everything we asked for.'

Prepare several stories about successes you have had. You can then select one that best fits the situation and puts you and/or your organisation in a good light. Keep it to no more than three to four sentences. Be clear about the point of the story, and use vivid language and an upbeat tone to make it memorable.

What is your exit strategy?

Many people feel uncomfortable breaking away from a conversation, even when it has obviously run its course. They do not want to seem rude, so they stand and talk some more – even though both people would rather move on. Do not allow being 'nice', considerate and thoughtful to hold you back. It is easier than you think to make an exit. Often people will feel the same and be glad you took the initiative.

10 top tips for exiting with grace

1 **Avoid the usual excuses**: People can see through them: going to the toilet, getting a drink or food.

2 **Never leave someone alone**: They will sometimes feel 'dumped'. Only leave them when you have no choice, such as when you have promised to talk to someone and you are running out of time.

3 **Check reactions**: Look at your partner's body language for signs of them wanting to move on. They could be itching for a change too.

4 **Possible exit lines if you are *sure* they are ready to move on**: 'I am sure you would like to circulate ... it was a pleasure to meet you.'

5 **Pass them on**: Offer to introduce your partner to someone you know who may be useful to them.

6 **Get them to pass you on**: Do they know anyone it would be useful for you to meet?

7 **Suggest you join another group**: 'Shall we go and meet some new people?'

8 **Don't just 'slip away' from a large group**: Say goodbye, shake hands. Last impressions are as important as first impressions.

9 **Show appreciation before you leave**: 'I am so glad about ...', 'Your clients are lucky to have you so enthusiastic about ...'

10 **Simple etiquette works**: End with 'Nice to meet you. I hope you enjoy the rest of the event.'

'I'll never forget whatshername'

You will have more impact if you recall people's names and faces. Make an effort to repeat a name when you hear it the first time, use it in conversation and say it again when you leave. One trick is to associate the name or face with a memorable image, such as a celebrity or someone you know. Or think of an adjective with the same letter as the name, like Simple Simon. You could also show interest in their name, if it is interesting, asking how they got it or how it is spelled.

If you forget their name it is generally not a big deal – more often than not they have forgotten yours – and it will only become an issue if you want to keep in touch. At that point you will swap business cards, if you have them, or write down contact details. You will then have their name.

When should you hand out your business card? Only when you have a legitimate reason to do so – and rarely at the beginning of the conversation. Your aim during the conversation should be to create a rationale for maintaining contact, so the exchange seems entirely natural. 'I will make sure to send you that article I mentioned – let me have your details.' Ask if it is okay to write on the card, and note down your commitment so you don't forget. You might also want to jot down some brief comments about them, your conversation and their interests – plus what they look like. It will help you remember them more easily later.

If they don't volunteer a card you may not have built up enough rapport or they just do not see you as a potential contact. Don't force a card on anyone. That is one cast-iron, guaranteed way of making a negative impact. Your card is part of your image, so make sure yours are clean and presentable. Don't have them loose in a pocket – always look after them.

When do you follow up?

How soon should you contact someone again? Typically two to three days – anything sooner can make you seem too keen; any longer and you don't seem interested. Email? Phone? Either can work. It depends on them, the situation and what you discussed. It goes without saying that if you promised to do something or send something, you must do it – and do it as soon as possible. Think about your purpose. Have a hook to get their attention, and be thinking about what the next step is for you. Here are some ideas:

- Send information that is relevant to their interests and is engaging.
- Write an email when you see their organisation in the press.
- Introduce them to someone else.
- Suggest a meeting – over coffee or lunch.
- Ask for help with something specific – most people like to feel useful.
- Invite them to a social or professional event.

The Facebook revolution – online social networking

Increasingly technology is enabling us to communicate anywhere, anytime. Wherever you go people are exchanging short messages, making connections with far greater frequency than ever before. The meteoric rise of Facebook membership reflects the power of online social networking in recent years. In fact, many businesses have banned its use in working hours because it began to cause significant down time. People became hooked on internet messaging.

Business networks include Ecademy and LinkedIn, which attract 25 million professionals who want to connect with others they can trust. Users benefit from finding jobs, opportunities and referrals, as well as filling vacancies. Frequently old contacts get in touch. Check them out.

How often do you peruse reviews on Amazon or eBay? Have these encouraged you to contribute? Networking is also about sharing photos, music and video clips. Millions of blogs, online forums and discussion groups are emerging as virtual networks. You may never meet those you 'converse' with, but you can benefit enormously from shared information and opinions.

Reciprocity is key

Networking is about giving, not getting. The more generous you are, the more impact you will have. If you give to someone, they will want to give back – and if they don't, you will get payback from others in your network. The currency is not always cash. However, unless someone has a specific need that you can fulfil, build the relationship first.

> the more generous you are, the more impact you will have

The possibilities of what you can give are endless – expertise, contacts, ideas, access to information, skills, interests and a personality that makes you good to spend time with. Think of yourself as a resource. This is not directly about selling yourself.

Become a hub – put your networks in contact with each other. If you are generous with your contacts, people will naturally return the favour. What they don't need now, they may need later.

It is very, very simple: the more you network, the more impact you will have on more people.

Make an impact now

- Write up a plan – how will networking achieve your goals? Set your targets now.

- Be prepared – research, evaluate, know your pitch.

- Reciprocity is key – give generously.

- Keep in touch – that is more than lots of people do in professional networking.

Afterword

Making it happen – turning theory into action

'You control your future, your destiny.
What you think about comes about ...
Set in motion the process of becoming
the person you most want to be. Put
your future in good hands – your own.'

Mark Victor Hansen, motivational
speaker and author

We have covered an enormous amount of ground – and if you have followed us all the way, so have you. As you have progressed through this book you no doubt have assessed what personal impact means to you and what you need to do to change and grow. You now have a multitude of tools and techniques that will enable you to have more impact in any situation you find yourself in – from standing out in meetings, to building a higher profile at work, getting that job or hot date, making yourself instantly likeable, handling nerves on big occasions ... and many more.

You always *have* controlled your future, your destiny. Mark Victor Hansen is absolutely right. Only now – if you choose – you can take charge of it so that you have even more control. You have reached a choice point. Do you close the book and do nothing more? Or do you turn theory into action?

Unless you have only skim-read the book, you have probably done some, if not all, of the exercises. You may have talked about what you have learnt to your friends and colleagues, perhaps had debates and discussions on certain points. Maybe you have gone out and tested our suggestions to convince yourself they work. That means you have already started to shift your thinking, developed your awareness and, consciously or unconsciously, you are behaving in a different way.

So why waste your investment in time? Put the book on the shelf and tell yourself that you will do something soon. You deserve more – and in truth – it is not hard to get going. What you need to do is make the time to set yourself some goals and prioritise your actions. Make yourself accountable. Think about what might get in the way and what other resources you need to make progress. There is no time like the present to act. In fact, there is no time *but* the present.

What stops most people from taking charge is getting going in the first place. Old habits die hard. You may know your apologetic language or irritating mannerism gets in the way of impact, but doing something different takes effort at first. Like learning to drive, you have to think of each step – clutch down, accelerator up, gear stick shift, clutch up … Once you get the hang of it, the changes become easy. Do not give up if something does not work the first time you try it.

Experiment. You don't have to get everything right straight away, so try out our suggestions and see what works for you. It is important to practise new ideas. Real changes in behaviour come through experience. Believe in yourself and keep going – remember that you are worth it. You will soon be doing quite effortlessly, and unconsciously, what seemed strange to begin with. Once the momentum gets going, you will see the results for yourself. Each small step you take will lead to big changes.

> believe in yourself and keep going – remember that you are worth it

People with the most impact are those who are constantly learning, adjusting and growing – their personal wisdom and presence oozes out of them. You can stand out from the crowd and you owe it to yourself to be the best you can be. Imagine how much happier and more successful you will be personally and professionally when you are absolutely bursting with impact. Good luck!

Appendix: What next?

Training

Reading a book on the subject gives you a great platform to start from. But you may come to a point where it is helpful to practise and get feedback from experts by attending a training course. You can cover similar ground in a highly interactive way and you have a coach at your fingertips to help you with specific issues you want to focus on.

More recently, training providers have started to offer courses in this area. In our business, Speak First, we have three levels of impact courses which address various aspects of impact and help people at different levels in an organisation. Shop around on the internet and get hold of training directories to find a course that meets your needs. Some dating agencies promote courses to develop your social impact. There are even specific workshops on flirting.

Further reading

There are very few books promoted under the banner of personal impact which address many or all of the topics covered in this book. Several examine impact in relation to influencing, some look at personal presence, many look at how you can improve the way you communicate with others in general, and many cover ways to get ahead. We have listed a few that relate specifically to the concepts mentioned in this book in the Further reading section.

Further reading

Angier, Michael E., Pond, Sarah and Angier, Dawn (2004), *101 Best Ways to Get Ahead: Solid Advice from 101 of the World's Most Successful People* (Success Networks International)

Anthony, Dr Robert (1994), *The Ultimate Secrets of Total Self-Confidence* (G.P. Putnam's Sons)

Aristotle (reissue 1991), *The Art of Rhetoric* (Penguin Classics)

Baber, Anne (2002), *Make Your Contacts Count: Networking Know-how for Cash, Clients and Career Success* (Amacom)

Back, Ken and Back, Kate (1982), *Assertiveness at Work: A Practical Guide to Handling Awkward Situations* (McGraw-Hill)

Barker, Alan (2006) *How to Manage Meetings* (Kogan Page)

Bavister, Steve and Vickers, Amanda (2004), *Essential NLP* (Hodder Education)

Bavister, Steve and Vickers, Amanda (2007), *Presenting with impact and confidence* (Hodder Education)

Bayan, Richard (revised edition 2006), *Words that Sell: More Than 6,000 Entries to Help You Promote Your Products, Services, and Ideas* (McGraw-Hill Professional)

Beaver, Diana (1997), *Easy Being: Making Life as Simple and as Much Fun as Possible* (Useful Book Co.)

Boe, Anne and Youngs, Bettie B. (1989), *Is Your 'Net' Working?* (John Wiley)

Boyes, Carolyn (2005), *Body Language* (Collins)

Bradberry, Travis and Greave, Jean (2006), *Emotional Intelligence Quickbook: Everything You Need to Know to Put Your EQ to Work* (Simon & Schuster)

Bright, Jim and Earl, Joanne (2007), *Brilliant CV: What Employers Want to See and How to Say It* (Prentice Hall)

Brinkman, Dr Rick and Kirschner, Dr Rick (1994), *How to Deal with People You Can't Stand* (McGraw-Hill)

Carnegie, Dale (2007), *How to Win Friends and Influence People* (Vermilion)

Charvet, Shelle Rose (1997), *Words That Change Minds: Mastering the Language of Influence* (Kendall/Hunt Publishing Company)

Cialdini, Robert (revised edition 2007), *Influence: The Psychology of Persuasion* (HarperBusiness)

Cialdini, Robert (2008) *Yes! 50 Scientifically Proven Ways to be Persuasive* (Free Press)

Collett, Peter (2003), *The Book of Tells: How to Read People's Minds from their Actions* (Doubleday)

Constantine, Susannah and Woodall, Trinny (2003) *What Not to Wear* (Weiderfeld & Nicolson)

Dimitrius, Jo-Ellan and Mazzarella, Mark (2000), *Put Your Best Foot Forward* (Scribner)

D'Souza, Steven (2008) *Brilliant Networking* (Pearson Education)

Ekman, Paul (2007), *Emotions Revealed: Recognizing Faces and Feelings to Improve Communication and Emotional Life* (Owl Books)

Fisher, Donna and Vilas, Sandy (1994), *Power Networking: 55 Secrets for Personal and Professional Success* (Mountain Harbour Publications)

Gladwell, Malcolm (2006), *Blink: The Power of Thinking Without Thinking* (Penguin Books)

Goldstein, Noah J. Martin, Steve J. and Cialdini, Robert B. (2007), *Yes! 50 Secrets from the Science of Persuasion* (Profile Books)

Goleman, Daniel (1999), *Working with Emotional Intelligence* (Bloomsbury Publishing)

Goleman, Daniel (2007), *Social Intelligence: The New Science of Human Relationships* (Arrow Books)

Grad, Marcia (1986), *Charisma: How to Get That Special Magic* (Thorsons)

Grant-Williams, Renee (2002), *Voice Power* (Amacom)

Hall, Edward, T. (1988), *Silent Language* (Bantam Doubleday Dell Publishing Group)

Helmstetter, Shad (1991) *What to Say When You Talk to Yourself* (Thorsons)

Jay, Ros (2007), *Brilliant Interview: What Employers Want to Hear and How to Say It* (Prentice Hall)

Jeffers, Susan (2007), *Feel the Fear and Do It Anyway: How to Turn Your Fear and Indecision into Confidence and Action* (Vermilion)

Klein, Naomi (2001), *No Logo* (Flamingo)

Laborde, Genie Z. (1983), *Influencing with Integrity: Management Skills for Communication and Negotiation* (Syntony Publishing)

Lieberman, David J. (2001), *Get Anyone to do Anything* (St Martin's Press)

Lieberman, David J. (2007), *You Can Read Anyone: Never Be Fooled, Lied To, or Taken Advantage of Again* (Viter Press)

McKenna, Paul (2006), *Instant Confidence* (Bantam Press)

McNally, David and Speak, Karl D. (2002), *Be Your Own Brand: A Breakthrough Formula for Standing Out from the Crowd* (Berrett-Koehler Publishers)

Mehrabian, Albert (1981), *Silent Messages: Implicit Communication of Emotions and Attitudes* (Wadsworth Publishing)

Montoya, Peter and Vandehey, Tim (2005), *The Personal Branding Phenomenon: The Ultimate Brand-Building and Business Development Handbook to Transform Anyone into an Indispensable Personal Brand* (Personal Branding Press)

Mosvick, Roger and Nelson, Robert (1996) *We've Got to Start Meeting Like This!* (Park Avenue Productions)

Neenan, Michael and Dryden, Windy (2001), *Life Coaching: A Cognitive Behavioural Approach* (Brunner-Routledge)

Nelson, Noelle C. (1998), *Winning!: Using Lawyers' Courtroom Techniques To Get Your Way in Everyday Situations* (Prentice Hall)

Pease, Allan and Barbara (2004), *The Definitive Book of Body Language* (Orion)

Rackham, Neil (1995) *SPIN Selling* (Gower Publishing)

RoAne, Susan (1988), *How to Work a Room* (Shapolcky Publishers)

Robbins, Anthony (1988), *Unlimited Power* (Simon & Schuster)

Sanders, Tim (2006), *The Likeability Factor: How to Boost Your L-Factor and Achieve Your Life's Dreams* (Three Rivers Press)

Smith, Manuel J. (1975) *When I Say No, I Feel Guilty: How to Cope – Using the Skills of Systematic Assertive Therapy* (Bantam)

Spillane, Mary (2000), *Branding Yourself: How to Look, Sound and Behave Your Way to Success* (Pan Books)

Thompson, Geoff (2007) *Fear: The Friend of Exceptional People* (Summersdale Publishers)

Triplett, Jan F. (1986), *Networker's Guide to Success: Or How Good Guys Can Finish First* (Turnkey Documents)

Whitworth, Laura, Kimsey-House, Henry, Kimsey-House, Karen and Sandahl, Philip (2007), *Co-Active Coaching: New Skills for Coaching People Toward Success in Work and Life* (Davies-Black Publishing)

Index